urban sprawl, which would eventually grow to envelop all of the smaller communities and land outside of the red line, had yet to start.

The
GOLDEN AGE
of
LONDON'S RAILWAYS
from
OLD POSTCARDS

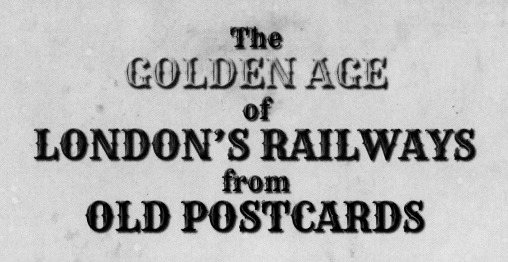

This early District Railway card was one of a set of six by the artist R. Joust. It would have been sold for one penny from a slot machine on one of the District's stations, in this case pre-stamped with an orange halfpenny. It specifically advertises Mansion House, which was the District station nearest to St. Paul's. Dating from circa 1898, it had an undivided back for the address only, with the blank space on the front intended for any message, and was what is known as 'court size' – about two thirds the size of the then British postcard standard of 5^1/$_2$ inches by 3^1/$_2$ inches. The card was printed using the chromo-lithographic process, which produced very vivid and attractive colours. DIST-802

A lot of lines and a lot of trains means a lot of signals! This is the London & South Western Railway's Waterloo 'A' box, photographed in 1908 during modernisation, with the new box on the right where the gantry has been extended, while on the left is the old box, which would soon be removed. The gantry holds six three-doll brackets, with twenty-three semaphore arms controlling arrivals and two more – the highest – for departures. These two indicated to an outgoing train whether it was routed to the main line (left) or Windsor line (right) and the height of all of the signals ensured that they were visible over the signal cabin. The picture was also published in the *South Western Gazette*, the L&SWR's staff magazine, in December 1908.

The GOLDEN AGE of LONDON'S RAILWAYS from OLD POSTCARDS

HENRY GUEST

JOHN ALSOP

Horse-drawn transport to the fore outside the North London Railway's Broad Street terminus, on an 'Oilette' card by Raphael Tuck in their 'London Railway Stations' Series II . Note the pair of covered double steps providing access to the platforms, which were at the higher level – not a welcome sight for the city gentleman hurrying for his train on the way home from work. It is possible that they also proved something of a deterrent to the Edwardian photographer with his cumbersome equipment, as interior views of the station are notoriously rare. The station was completely demolished following closure and the site now lies under the huge Boadgate retail and office development.

BROAD STREET STATION (LONDON).

Just west of Hammersmith on the District Railway's line is Ravenscourt Park, where an anonymous photographer neatly captured one of the Great Western Railway's trains, probably on a Richmond to Ladbroke Grove service, which had operated from 1st January 1894. The view is taken from the north side of the line, which had initially been opened on 1st January 1879 by the London & South Western Railway, and the photographer was in Ravenscourt Park. Posted in December 1907, the weather looks about right for the sundial on the left, so was clearly taken a few months earlier.

Published by LIGHTMOOR PRESS
© Lightmoor Press & John Alsop 2018
Designed by Neil Parkhouse

British Library Cataloguing-in-Publication Data. A catalogue record for this book is available from the British Library

ISBN: 9781911038 35 1

LIGHTMOOR PRESS
Unit 144B, Lydney Trading Estate, Harbour Road, Lydney, Gloucestershire GL15 4EJ
www.lightmoor.co.uk
Lightmoor Press is an imprint of Black Dwarf Lightmoor Publications Ltd

Printed in Poland
www.lfbookservices.co.uk

Contents

Preface . . . . page 7

Introduction . . . . page 8

The Postcard Publishers . . . . page 9

1 Euston L&NWR . . . . page 11

2 St. Pancras MR . . . . page 23

3 King's Cross GNR . . . . page 33

4 Broad Street NLR . . . . page 49

5 Liverpool Street GER . . . . page 61

6 Fenchurch Street GER, LT&SR and MDR . . . . page 75

7 Cannon Street and Charing Cross SER . . . . page 79

8 Holborn Viaduct and Blackfriars LC&DR . . . . page 87

9 Victoria and London Bridge LB&SCR . . . . page 99

10 Waterloo L&SWR . . . . page 113

11 Paddington GWR . . . . page 129

12 Marylebone GCR . . . . page 141

13 West London Line GWR & L&NWR Joint . . . . page 147

14 Underground Lines . . . . page 151

15 Exhibitions . . . . page 183

16 Industrial Railways . . . . page 189

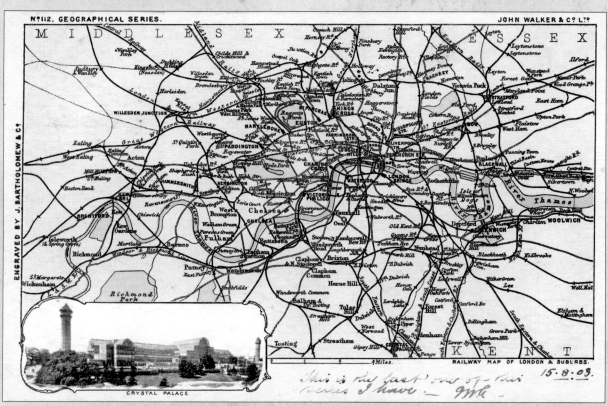

Card No. 112 of John Walker & Co. Ltd's Geographical Series, which covered much of the country, shows the railways of London with an inset of the Crystal Palace. Quite an early series of postcards, this one was posted on 13th August 1903 and gives a good overall idea of the tangle of lines that comprised London's railways at the period we are looking at, with the places we will be visiting all within the area shown.

'London Life' was a popular theme with Edwardian postcard publishers – series of cards depicting the various trades and occupations that could be encountered when walking or travelling around the capital. The Rotary Photographic Company's fascinating series of 'London Life' pictures was the largest of these, running to ninety-nine cards; this is No. 49 'Underground Tube Train Conductor'. This excellent photograph enables us to see *'Underground'* embroidered on his labels and his number, 972, on his cap badge but nothing else can be made out. Note the use of gates at the end of carriages – no sliding doors yet. What little that can be seen of the carriage looks as though it belongs to the Central London Railway and the date is about 1910.

10513—49   ROTARY PHOTO, E.C.
LONDON LIFE. UNDERGROUND TUBE TRAIN CONDUCTOR.

Preface
How Did It All Begin?

The very start was probably in the summer of 1941, when at a young age I could be found racing trains starting for the north from Church Stretton station. And my very first memory of a postcard was having a coloured one on my birthday that year. Collecting started with engine numbers, Ian Allan's 1945 LMS ABC being a real eye-opener. But collecting cards came a while later, when I found a Glasgow & South Western Railway official in a family album.

I was already by that time good friends with the Casserleys (I met Richard at school in 1945) and when I showed my find to him I was immediately invited to see other officials and was given some spares. That was in the mid-1950s and certainly by 1960 I was well immersed!

Originally I concentrated on officials and worked at producing a 'complete' listing with help from a number of the older brethren of railway enthusiasts. A typed listing appeared in 1968, which looks very thin when compared with what is now known fifty years on.

I was fortunate enough to move into computers in 1967 and soon found ways to record all the information I was gathering. An improved listing of officials was produced and I passed a copy to a fellow collector, who set about publishing the information. Only the first two volumes ever appeared, so I decided to put it all together as a complete extensively illustrated volume which resulted in self-publication of *The Official Railway Postcard Book** in 1987 (a few copies still available). Since then much more information has come to light and the listings are now available in a series of checklists, A5 size booklets, which also cover the main series of commercial railway cards such as Tuck Oilettes.

Interest spread well beyond the officials and embraced stations and other related cards, and also certain publishers of photographic locomotive and train cards. This probably followed on from various photographic safaris with the Casserleys (usually in the unheated pre-war Hillman – great in winter!) and I started working with Richard on various projects. Initially this was LM&SR coaching stock but we then moved on to The Locomotive Publishing Company (LPC) and the cards of E. Pouteau, with examples from both publishers featuring in this volume.

Although neither will ever be complete, there now exists on computer comprehensive lists of these cards, along with those of H. Gordon Tidey.

The work on LPC resulted in a database for the National Railway Museum, and the Pouteau information appeared in serial form in the Lightmoor Press journal *Railway Archive*. A regular feature I also produced for *Railway Archive* was under the title of 'Wish You Were Here?', based on picture postcards, which led on to the idea for this volume.

I now try to share the collection as widely as possible and pictures from it have appeared in numerous magazines and books, together with a few on television. Thanks should in particular go to Neil Parkhouse who has been responsible for publishing many and who has done a great job putting this volume together. There are many others, past and present, who have helped in many ways, to whom thanks are due.

It is possible that much of this would not have happened if it were not for the support I received from my late wife, Barbara, who was also a collector but of plants, having almost 600 different daylilies. These I keep going in her memory.

If you are interested in any of the publications mentioned above then please contact me by email:
john.alsop@btinternet.com.

John Alsop, Gloucestershire 2018

RAILWAY POSTCARD CHECKLISTS
OFFICIAL POSTCARDS
1. Caledonian and Highland Railways
2. London & North Western Railway
2A. LNWR Official Overprints
3. LMS, Midland, Northern Counties Committee, and North Stafford Railways
4. Maryport & Carlisle, Furness, Lancs & Yorks, Glasgow & South Western, Portpatrick, Stratford on Avon & Midland Junction, Wirral, West Coast, and Barrow Steam Navigation
5. Great Central, Great Eastern, Great Northern, North Eastern, East Coast, and Hull & Barnsley Railways
6. Great North of Scotland, North British, West Highland, and London & North Eastern Railways
7. Barry, Cambrian, Corris, Great Western, and Vale of Rheidol Railways
8. Southern Railway and constituents, and Early London Views
8A. The French Railways Poster cards
9. Irish and Isle of Man Railways, Snowdon, and other minor British Railways; The London Underground Railways
15. British Railways Officials, 1948-Privatisation, including Sealink and Hotels

GENERAL POSTCARDS
10. Commercial Coloured Railway Postcards 1902-c.1960, excluding Locomotive Publishing Company, Alpha, Tilling and Ian Allan
10A. Commercial Coloured Railway Postcards, 1897-c.1960, Locomotive Publishing Company, Alpha, Tilling and Ian Allan
11. Ravenglass & Eskdale Railway to 1960
12. Black & White Commercial Railway Postcards to 1953. Part 1: Locomotive Publishing Company
13. Black and White Commercial Railway Postcards to c.1960. Part 2: Miscellaneous Publishers including Mack, Pouteau, Smith, Sweetman, Valentine, W.&K. Wrench
14. Stations and other cards of Railway Interest by Kingsway, Charles Martin, Chapman, Fred Spalding
All £2.50 each, except 2A £2.00; P&P: 1–3 copies = 50p; 4–12 copies = £2.00; 13 or more = £3.00
The Official Railway Postcard Book £20.00 + £5.50 p&p

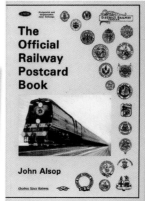

Introduction

An Exploration of London's Railways through Picture Postcards

In Great Britain, the picture postcard was authorised for use by the Post Office in September 1894. It took a while to catch on and become popular, not helped by the fact that for several years any message could only be written on the picture side, which today is generally referred to as the front, with the blank reverse to be used only for the address. However, in 1902, regulations changed and the 'divided back' appeared, which allowed the left half to be used for correspondence and the right for the address, which left the front to be used for the picture alone.

This change led to the 'Golden Age' of the picture postcard, which it is generally agreed lasted through the Edwardian era and up until the Great War, and it is mainly through this period that our tour of London's railways takes place. The earliest card shown dates from 1896, while there are just a couple into the 1920s, when the Grouping of the early railway companies in to the 'Big Four' – the Great Western Railway, the London, Midland & Scottish Railway, the London & North Eastern Railway and the Southern Railway – took place. The cards contained within these pages thus celebrate the pre-Grouping era on the railways, a colourful age when locomotives and carriages were generally painted and lined out in magnificent liveries designed to emphasise their design and the ambitions of their owning companies.

In general, therefore, although we begin at the end of the Victorian age and finish during the rather bleak period that followed the end of the First World War, it is the Edwardian Age that we are seeing, which was very much a time of change. Motor vehicles were coming and the horse-drawn trams were being superceded by those running on electricity. As a result, the railways were coming under serious competition from trams and motor buses in urban areas, and particularly in London.

In these early years of the 20th century, the telephone was still in its infancy but with perhaps four or five postal deliveries during the day in the major cities, the postcard was the way to send messages that could even relate to meetings the same evening. There is a well recounted tale of a city banker in the first decade of the century who used to arrive at his desk at 8.00am, take a look at his schedule for the day and then send a postcard to his wife in the suburbs telling her what time to expect him home for dinner! In fact, it is likely that many made use of this facility. Telegrams were of course an alternative but were more expensive and tended to be used more for emergencies. Few people had phones, unlike today, and in some of the pictures you will see a sign 'YOU MAY TELEPHONE FROM HERE', a feature which lasted at many rural stations in to the 1950s.

The tour will in general look at the lines relating to each of the London termini in turn, beginning with the London & North Western Railway's iconic terminus at Euston and then working clockwise from there. However, London's railways formed a complex network and it is necessary to jump around

a little in the outer areas. The geographic coverage is also restricted to the central area of the capital, within a radius of approximately 7 miles of Charing Cross.

Some of the scenes are pure railway and from cards produced for the enthusiast market, while at the other end of the scale are groups of workers on cards that were probably produced in very limited numbers for the subjects and their families. Between these extremes are the many views of stations, inside and outside, which give a great insight to life at the time. There are also a good selection of cards that were produced by the railway companies' themselves – 'official' cards as they are termed within the postcard collecting fraternity. Some of the railways embraced this new medium for promotion far more than others, the greatest exponent of all being the London & North Western Railway, who issued hundreds of different card designs in scores of different sets, many of which were published in millions. For these official cards, the Alsop reference number is given at the end of the caption (see Checklists).

So far as it is possible, dates are given for when the cards first appeared, together with the name of the original publisher but the dating of many is far from being an exact science. The style of card and reference on it to regulations can give a fair idea of when it was published, whilst postmarks provide a latest date. With a local photographer/publisher, it was above all the case that cards were often produced very soon after the picture was taken but with large national or international companies pictures could be years older, coming from extensive libraries. Real photographic cards – deemed to be those produced directly from the original glass plate or negative – showing special events could even be on sale the same day.

A good number of the stations to be visited are still in use today but modernisation of the railways has seen many of the original buildings go, designs of style and distinction often being replaced with dreadful bus shelter-type structures. In capturing this vanished age and the railway that went with it, there is much to look at on these cards and it can be very rewarding to take time to study them.

PUBLISHER'S NOTE: It has been our aim to reproduce most of the postcards featured within these pages as closely as we can to how they look to collectors. Sepia toning was a far from exact science and whilst many mastered the art, many more skimped on the expensive chemicals involved, with the result that many photographic cards faded soon after printing – not as a result of prolonged exposure to direct sunlight as many believe – and here the redoubtable E. Pouteau was as culpable as any. It also explains the wide range of sepia tones to be found on display here. Computer programmes can now dramatically enhance the image from faded cards, 'hoover' out damage suffered or detritus accumulated in the hundred plus years since they were printed, or adjust the toning, so a few of the cards seen here have been 'improved' in this way but the vast majority have been reproduced exactly as they appear.

The Postcard Publishers

Without the efforts of the postcard publishers, it would not have been possible to produce this book so they are acknowledged by these details. In a number of cases only initials are known, not all have addresses and quite a few of the cards were published anonymously.

Appleby Series
Austin, 24 Joley Street, London W.
Beagles, J. & Co. Ltd, London, E.C.
Bell's Photo Co. Ltd, Leigh-on-Sea, Essex.
Blum & Degen Ltd, London
Card House, 84 Rye Lane, S.E.
Clarke, E.F.
D. & Co.
D. & D.
D. & M.
Daily Mail
Davidson Bros, London & New York
Dederich, W., Imperial Buildings, Ludgate Circus, London, E.C.
Downer, Watford
Dukes, R.E., 3 Barnsbury Street, Upper Street, Islington, N.
E.& C.G.
Eyre & Spottiswoode, The Woodbury Series
Folkes J., 3 Packington Street, Islington, N.
Fullers Photo Series
G.D. & D.L.
Giesen Bros & Co., London E.C. (for CLR)
Groom, B.W., 22 Trumpington Street, Cambridge
H.M. & Co., London
H.M. & S.L.
H.R.M.
Hagelberg, W., London, New York, Berlin
Hampden Photo-Printing Co. 99 Hampden Road, Hornsey
Hartmann
Hutchinson & Co, Wimbledon
John's Series
Lane, S., 14 Catford Hill, S.E.
Levy Freres, Paris (LL)
Libraire Continentale, 3 Wilton Road, London, S.W.
Locomotive Publishing Co. Ltd, 3 Amen Corner, London E.C.
Marquis, W.D.
Martin, Charles, 39 Aldermanbury, London, E.C.
McCorquodale & Co. Ltd
Etablissements Photographiques de Neuerdein Freres, Paris (ND)
Nevill, W.H., 159 Fortess Road, N.W.
Oliver Arc Lamp Ltd
P. & S.
P.S. & V. Lewisham
Perkins & Son, Lewisham
Perryer, W.H., 14 Loxwood Road, Tottenham N.
Photochrom Co. Ltd, London
Pictorial Postcard Syndicate Limited, 73 Moorgate Street, London EC

Picture Postcard Company Ltd, 6 Draper's Gardens, E.C.
Pouteau, E., 231a Gray's Inn Road, King's Cross, W.C.
R.P. Co., London. Collotone Series
Reeve
Rotary Photo E.C.
Rush & Warwick, Bedford
Saffra, Geo., Tottenham
Secretan, G.W., 210A Tufnell Park Road, N.
Serjeant, 159 Ladbroke Grove, W.
Smith G., 15 Stroud Green, N.
Smith Premier Typewriter Co., Ltd, 6 and 7 Queen Street, London, E.C.
Stengel, O.F. & Co. Ltd, London N.
Taylor, A. & G., 70 Queen Victoria Street, London E.C. Reality Series
Tempertons Stationery Stores, Fulham
Tidey, H. Gordon, 2 Ullswater Road, Southgate
Tuck, Raphael & Sons
Walker, John & Co., London (Bell's Series)
Waterlow & Sons Ltd (for LB&SCR)
Watts, G.H.
W.H. Smith & Sons Ltd (Kingsway Series)
Wrench, E., The Wrench Series
Wyman

To avoid a lot of repetition of the railway names abbreviations are used in many cases.

CCE&HR	Charing Cross, Euston & Hampstead Railway
CLR	Central London Railway (The 'Twopenny Tube')
C&SLR	City & South London Railway
DR	District Railway
GCR	Great Central Railway
GER	Great Eastern Railway
GN&CR	Great Northern & City Railway
GNP&BR	Great Northern, Piccadilly & Brompton Railway
GWR	Great Western Railway
H&CR	Hammersmith & City Railway
LB&SCR	London, Brighton & South Coast Railway
LC&DR	London, Chatham & Dover Railway
LM&SR	London, Midland & Scottish Railway
L&NWR	London & North Western Railway
L&SWR	London & South Western Railway
MET	Metropolitan Railway
MR	Midland Railway
NLR	North London Railway
SE&CR	South Eastern & Chatham Railway
SER	South Eastern Railway
T&HJR	Tottenham & Hampstead Joint Railway
WLER	West London Extension Railway
WLR	West London Railway

ENTRANCE TO EUSTON STATION.
L. & N.W. RAILWAY

The entrance to Euston station was guarded and dominated by the massive Doric Arch, an iconic structure designed by the architect Philip Hardwick and built by the London & Birmingham Railway in 1837. Demolished during the rebuilding of the station in 1961-2, to a huge outcry at the loss of such an historic piece of early railway infrastructure, much of the stone was subsequently discovered in the River Lea by the historian Dan Cruickshank in 1994, who established a trust a couple of years later dedicated to its rebuilding. More of the stone has since been located at properties of those involved in its demolition and there are firm plans to rebuild it as part of the new High Speed 2 railway line. Ironically – and perhaps predictably – following completion of the rebuilding of Euston station in the later 1960s, it was found that there would have been room for the arch to have remained in place. Dating from 1907, this official L&NWR card is looking across a busy Euston Road, with a fine selection of horse-drawn transport on view, including a couple of Hansom cabs in the foreground, a Brougham on the right and a delivery cart in the background. The Euston Hotel can be seen through the arch. LNW-436.

ENTRANCE TO EUSTON STATION, FROM EUSTON ROAD.

On the Left is a view of WEST LODGE ENQUIRY and BOOKING OFFICE, which is conveniently situated for passengers arriving by bus from all parts of London.

In the background is the EUSTON HOTEL, one of the most comfortable Hotels in London. It contains 300 Rooms; is lighted throughout by Electricity and fitted with Passenger Lifts to each floor. Large and spacious DINING, DRAWING, and RECEPTION ROOMS, etc., and also several well appointed PRIVATE SUITES OF ROOMS available for Public Meetings. Theatre Ticket Bureaux in the Vestibule, and Messrs. Wyman & Sons' Library in the Front Hall. Telephonic communication from the Halls and from each floor to all parts of England and the Metropolis

LEFT & BELOW: This view of Euston station from Euston Road is on one of the London & North Western Railway official postcards and as the view of the reverse shows, carried a notation in the stamp space stating '*Over 8½ millions sold*', which dates the card to 1908 or 1909. There is plenty of information about the hotel below the picture and the correspondence space on the back is filled with the list of L&NWR refreshment rooms, those at forty-four stations being listed. LNW-952.

1
EUSTON
London
& North
Western
Railway

RIGHT: Having passed under the arch, the prospective traveller came into the station courtyard, where their cab would bring them to the departure side, which was protected by a glazed covered roof. The card dates again from 1907 and all traffic is still horse-drawn; in particular, note the Royal Mail dray on the right. This is one of the wide range of subjects included by the L&NWR on their official postcards. LNW-440.

THE COURTYARD, EUSTON STATION

EUSTON HOTEL LONDON

LEFT: From the same period is another L&NWR official card, showing the frontage of the hotel we have just read about. This is the view from the station side, with what used to be the Victoria Hotel on the left and Euston Hotel on the right. The construction of the linking block and the change to the single name of Euston Hotel took place in 1881. The hotel closed on 13th May 1963 and was subsequently demolished, along with all of the other buildings at Euston station that are shown in these views. LNW-800.

Standing at the inner end of Platform 1, the photographer of this view obtained a fine shot of the arrival side of Euston station. There are not many people on the platform, suggesting that the train had arrived some minutes previously. The numberplate on the engine is not very clear but it is probably No. 1668, which was a 'Precedent' Class 2-4-0 carrying the name *Dagmar*. Built in May 1891, this engine was in service for over forty years until it was scrapped in 1933. The postcard, No. 199 in the Collotone Series by R.P. Co., dates from about 1904. We shall see some nicely tinted cards through these pages but this is not one of them! Here, colour has been applied by means of a rough wash, using the three primary shades but each in a specific area; fortunately, this has not obscured any of the detail.

Euston Station L. & N. W. R. Interior

LPC No. 4275 in the *Locomotive Magazine Series* shows Great Northern Railway 'Atlantic' No. 1449 at Euston in June 1910, when it ran some trials on the L&NWR. The Chief Mechanical Engineers of the various railways would have been members of the same professional bodies, where they would meet and discuss progress and new ideas. Occasionally this would result in trials of an engine on the other company's lines, quite often on a swap basis. Some lovely detail on the signals in the foreground; several of the arms have a ring, which on the L&NWR denoted that they were for the slow (relief) lines.

No doubts at all regarding the date of this picture, October 5th 1910. A bevy of Birmingham and Midland Grocers – as noted on the board on the front of the engine but probably in fact from the Birmingham & Midland Counties Grocers Protection & Benevolent Association – pose for the photographer by a very much decorated locomotive, an unidentified member of the 'Precursor' Class. If the decorations were carried all the way from Birmingham the train must have been quite a sight and provided excellent publicity for Mazawattee Tea. The company was founded in 1887 and at this date had a large factory alongside the Grand Surrey Canal at New Cross, with head offices at Tower Hill, near the Tower of London. The train would have been a special laid on by the Mazawattee Company as a thank you to retailers in the Midlands area for stocking their brand, with a tour of the factory and no doubt a grand luncheon included. The picture propped against the locomotive's smokebox, a painting of a grandmother and grand-daughter with a pot of tea, was the company's main advertising illustration for many years. However, whilst all the paraphernalia decorating the engine is genuine, the 'MAZAWATTEE SPECIAL' sign top right has the appearance of being an addition to the original photograph. The company was sold in 1953, its factory and offices having been largely destroyed by bombing during the Second World War, and its trading name ceased to be used soon after. Note the sign pointing to 'PUBLIC TELEPHONES IN LARGE HALL'. The location of course is Euston but the card is otherwise anonymous.

LOADING BAGGAGE INTO·AMERICAN SPECIAL. EUSTON.

ABOVE: Another card from the *Locomotive Magazine Series*, No. 2714, shows the view looking into Euston with the arrival platforms to the left, the local platforms placed centrally and main line departures to the right. The driver would need to know exactly where he was heading from the signals which would be controlling his progress.

LEFT: The American Special which ran from Euston to the Riverside station at Liverpool was seen by the L&NWR as a most prestigious train. This 1906 postcard shows an often neglected side of running a service like this. Travellers who were making a transatlantic voyage would always have much luggage, that also had to be loaded and transported. This is the scene at Euston station, probably Platform 13, prior to departure. LNW-434

RIGHT: Raphael Tuck published two sets of cards of London stations in 1906, Series No. 9279 in March and No. 9383 in December. It is generally agreed that the colours on them are reasonably accurate, which makes this view of Euston most interesting, with a Cambrian Railways carriage in the left foreground; this is the only good contemporary view in colour of a Cambrian carriage. We are on the main departure platforms and looking to the north but there is clearly no rush and there is time to study what the well dressed Edwardian wore to travel.

EUSTON STATION. L&N.W.R.

In late 1906, when this postcard was published, there was some serious competition between the L&NWR and the Great Western Railway. The latter were looking at ways of reducing the distance to Birmingham from Paddington (at the time the 'Great Way Round' via Didcot and Oxford), so the L&NWR wanted as firm a hold as they could on the Birmingham traffic before the GWR could introduce their faster trains, which would eventually happen in 1910. This wonderful poster, reproduced by the L&NWR as a postcard, was one of the results. The card was even subsequently amended and reissued to reflect the change of time to two of the trains. The version shown here is the original issue and copies may be found with the times amended by hand before the reprint was produced. LNW-744A

'Alfred the Great' Class 4-4-0 No. 1973 *Hood* stands awaiting departure from Euston while staff pose for the photographer. *Hood* was built in July 1903, rebuilt to 'Renown' Class in 1921 and was scrapped in 1926, never carrying its allocated LM&SR No. 5175. The photograph was by H. Gordon Tidey and could well depict the important two-hour Birmingham train due to depart at 2.30 in the afternoon, as shown on the poster card above.

RIGHT: The view here dates from around 1902 and shows 1899-built 'Alfred the Great' Class No. 1916 *Irresistible* waiting to leave Euston with a train bound for Scotland. The caption on the card states it is leaving but the signals suggest that this is not in fact the case, as they are all at danger. It is worth remembering that Edwardian postcard captions were not always correct. The card was published some years later, in 1907, by the Locomotive Publishing Co. The advertisements on the right include signs for Vickers Inks, Suttons Seeds, Keen's Mustard and one titled Books & Blessings!

10 a. m. Scotch Express leaving Euston Station.

LEFT: Another view of a Scotch Express leaving Euston but this time it is clearly signalled for departure. This is also by the LPC and is one of the fine coloured cards by F. Moore. These pictures were produced by painting directly onto photographs, thus ensuring technical accuracy. Great trouble was taken and, again, it has always been considered that the colours are correct. The engine is 'Precursor' Class No. 659 *Dreadnought*, which was built in June 1904. Rebuilt to 'George V' Class in 1915, the 4-4-0 survived to May 1936.

RIGHT: Whilst generally known for producing local view cards of the Hertfordshire area, Downer of Watford did cover a few stations and other scenes of railway interest. This is perhaps one of his best, after he had been allowed access into the No. 2 cabin at Euston, the photographer making a good job of capturing the grand array of levers – two rows of them. However, it is not known whether Downer took the photograph himself or whether he was supplied with official pictures by the railway company. The card was posted in November 1905.

No 2 SIGNAL CABIN, EUSTON. L. & N.W. RY.

Published by the LPC in 1905, No. 1422 in their *Locomotive Magazine Series*, the photograph actually dates from a few years earlier. The scene is at Camden locomotive shed, situated just over a mile from the terminus and that provided engines for services from Euston as well as for the Camden goods depot, which was just on the opposite side of the line here. On the left is 'Special Tank' No. 3156, which had carried this duplicate list number since May 1892. There are two of the 'Problem' Class 'Singles' in the centre and what look to be 'Dreadnought' 2-2-2-0s on the right. However, there is no sign of any 'Jubilees', which came into service from 1899, suggesting a date of circa 1898-99 for the picture. The turntable seen here in the left foreground had been removed by about 1910. Chalk Farm station was situated next to the shed and it is just possible to glimpse the platforms to the right of the shed building. Opened as Hampstead Road in 1855, it was renamed Chalk Farm in December 1862 and had platforms serving the main line to and from Euston and the North London line. However, the main line platforms were closed in 1915, the station thereafter being served solely by trains running between Watford Junction and Broad Street. Renamed Primrose Hill by British Railways (BR) in September 1950, the station was closed completely in 1992, by which time the once a day service was terminating at Liverpool Street, following the closure of Broad Street in 1986.

Kilburn Station and High Road, Kilburn.

Dating probably from 1907, this anonymous view of Kilburn High Road fortuitously included the station. The L&NWR signboard over the entrance also advised that there was a 'UNIVERSAL GOODS AND PARCELS BOOKING OFFICE' here. Two horse cabs stand in front of the station, while an early motor bus, registration No. LC6765, heads for Cricklewood. The policeman seems to have something in his eye or perhaps he was saluting the photographer! Note to his right the sign for a PUBLIC TELEPHONE. The exterior of the station is completely changed but some of the buildings on the right remain.

Two miles from Euston, the station at Kilburn & Maida Vale had four platforms and was originally served by local trains on the main line. This all changed with the introduction of electric trains using DC conductor rails (so as to be compatible with the underground) in 1912, which used the old slow line platforms, just glimpsed in the right background. Semi-fast services then used the old main line platforms, with the main lines being diverted to the south to miss the station altogether. The station was opened as Kilburn in December 1851, being renamed Kilburn & Maida Vale on 1st June 1879. It was closed from 1st January 1917 as part of the war-time economies, reopening on 10th July 1922, with a further renaming shortly after, on 1st August 1923, when it became Kilburn High Road. This view was taken in 1914 or 1915 by H. Gordon Tidey, who captured an unidentified 'Renown' Class drifting through the old main line platforms on the last stage of its journey to Euston. The station is still open as Kilburn High Road today but only the slow line platforms remain, the semi fast line platforms being removed during the electrification of this section of the West Coast Main Line in the 1960s.

LUNCHEON BASKETS

are supplied to passengers in the trains at the **EUSTON**, Willesden, Kensington (Addison Road), Bletchley, Northampton, Rugby, Coventry, Nuneaton, Stafford, Hereford, Carlisle, Shrewsbury, Builth Road, Crewe, Birmingham, Wolverhampton, Liverpool, Stockport, Manchester (Exchange and London Road Stations), Chester, Llandudno Junction, Bangor, Holyhead, Wigan, Preston, and Lancaster Stations, and **HOT Luncheons,** consisting of fillet of beef or mutton chop, fried potatoes, bread, &c., at the same charge, are supplied at Preston, Crewe, Rugby, Stafford, and Northampton (Castle). When hot luncheons are required, notice must be given to the guard of the train at the preceding stopping station.

POST CARD

Buy the L. & N. W. Series of Pictorial Postcards. 2d. per set of six different cards. Over 8¼ millions sold.

(FOR ADDRESS ONLY.)

WILLESDEN STATION.

WILLESDEN JUNCTION is one of the busiest Junctions in the three Kingdoms. In addition to the trains calling here *en route* to Scotland, Holyhead (for Ireland), Wales, Liverpool, Manchester, and Birmingham, etc., there are numerous suburban connections, the principal ones being to Mansion House, Broad Street, Dalston, Highbury (for the Agricultural Hall), Victoria (for the Continent), Kew Gardens, Richmond, Kensington (Addison Road for the West End and Olympia), Chelsea (for the grounds of the famous Chelsea Football Club which adjoin), Hampstead Heath, Camden Town or Chalk Farm (for the Zoological Gardens), **Earl's Court (for the Hungarian Exhibition), Uxbridge Road (covered entrance to the Franco-British Exhibition),** St. Quintin Park (for the Wood Lane Entrance to the Stadium).

LEFT & BELOW: The references to the exhibitions, which opened in May 1908, clearly puts the date of this L&NWR official card as 1908. At this period, Willesden Junction was an important station and many main line trains called there; the view shows a goods train on the left, a passenger service on the main line and a North London Railway Broad Street train in what were known as the North London Bay platforms to the right. Far right is a large carriage shed, empty coaches having to be worked the 5½ miles to Euston, there not being space for this any closer. Running right across in the background is the structure of the high level station serving the Broad Street to Richmond line and again the ringed signals, denoting that they referred to the slow lines. The main line station was closed and completely demolished as part of the 1960s electrification work. LNW-963.

WILLESDEN JUNCTION. L.&N.W.RY.   DOWNER, WATFORD.

LEFT: Assuming they were his own photographs, Mr Downer was allowed access to some interesting places, or perhaps he was supplied with pictures to use. This view was clearly taken from the signal box situated between the main line on the right and the West London Railway curving away to the left on its way to Clapham Junction. The short passenger train, hauled by an 'Alfred the Great' Class engine, is carrying an express headcode (one lamp each end of the buffer beam) and there looks to be a sleeping car in the carriage sidings on the right. The postcard is unused but dates from about 1905.

RIGHT: This is the road to the modern entrance to the 'New Line' platforms at Willesden Junction. The term 'New Line' was to differentiate them from the high level and main line platforms when those for the electric service came into use. Walking past here today, the building has gone and there is a view to the site of the long demolished main line platforms, whilst no longer is there this grand sign for the intending passenger to study. The station was a busy place and did indeed have services heading far and wide. The booking office seen here is thought to have been opened on 1st July 1891. Posted in March 1907, the card probably dates from 1904 and is No. 4 in the H.R.M. Series. The firm appears to have published in the north-west London area but has yet to be otherwise identified.

H. R. M., Series 4.   Willesden Junction Station.

LEFT: August 1910 saw exchange trials between a Great Western Railway 'Star' Class locomotive and an L&NWR 'Experiment'. It seems that the GWR engine proved superior and here the photographer was able to capture No. 4005 *Polar Star* passing through Willesden station on the 12.10pm Euston to Liverpool, Manchester & Birkenhead Luncheon Car express. Fitted with a superheater shortly after the exchange, No. 4005 lasted in service until November 1934. A bookstall is almost lost in the shadows beside the engine, whilst just to the left of the man on the platform is a copy of the L&NWR's famous 'Irish Golf Links' poster; this also was issued on card, LNW-742. The card shown here was published in the *Locomotive Magazine Series*, No. 3460.

ABOVE: An anonymous real photographic card of a building site posted in July 1911. The view is actually looking across the works at Willesden for the 'New Electric Railway' (this is the DC line referred to a couple of pages ago) and shows the site for the station. The booking office we saw at the bottom of the previous page is just off picture to the right, whilst the outline of the high level platforms runs across the middle of the picture. There does not seem to be much happening and even the three men working on the retaining wall have stopped for the photographer.

RIGHT: The card shown at the top of the next page was produced for company correspondence and this is the reverse. Although the front was London-related, it was actually sent from Longwood & Milnsbridge station, on the outskirts of Huddersfield, to Messrs Shaw & Shaw, textile manufacturers of Britannia Mills, Milnsbridge in September 1906. The cards were filed on receipt, hence the punch holes. LNW-811.

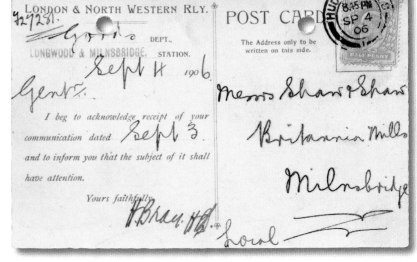

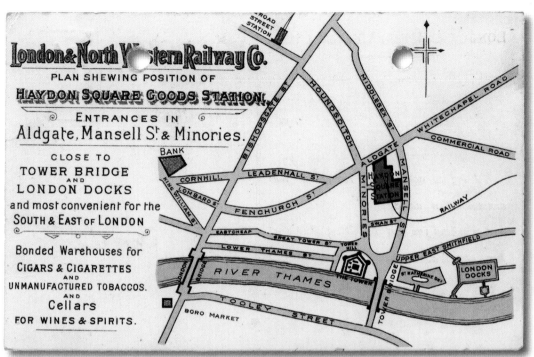

London & North Western Railway Co.

PLAN SHEWING POSITION OF

HAYDON SQUARE GOODS STATION.

ENTRANCES IN
Aldgate, Mansell St. & Minories.

CLOSE TO
TOWER BRIDGE
AND
LONDON DOCKS
and most convenient for the
SOUTH & EAST OF LONDON

Bonded Warehouses for
CIGARS & CIGARETTES
AND
UNMANUFACTURED TOBACCOS.
AND
Cellars
FOR WINES & SPIRITS.

LEFT: Tucked away at the east edge of the City of London was an outpost of the L&NWR at Haydon Square. The company produced this postcard (the reverse of which is shown at the bottom of the previous page) to acknowledge correspondence and to show exactly where their goods depot was situated but being a card for business use, it would not have been on sale to the public. Most would not have survived their usage for long and thus it is a very rare and much sought after item today. The depot is marked on an 1851 map so was in existence for over a hundred years but by the mid-1960s had become a car and lorry park. The area has since been totally redeveloped. LNW-811.

RIGHT: Hidden beneath the Haydon Square goods depot was a large bonded store, where goods liable to excise duty would have been held. This is another card produced by the L&NWR in 1906 and, as with the map above, was for use by the company (see scan of reverse, below top right). Thus, unlike the Euston cards already shown, it did not feature in any of the sets for sale to the public. LNW-751.

BELOW: It looks very much as though the photographer was in Apsley House for this picture of Hyde Park, looking down the Carriage Road left and Rotten Row to the right. Although not immediately apparent that it is railway related, the card was produced in 1906 or 1907 by the West Coast Royal Mail Route (see scan of reverse bottom right below), the joint operation between the L&NWR and the Caledonian Railway to operate the top Anglo-Scottish expresses. There was even special rolling stock for this and the card was for correspondence use by Caledonian Railway offices in Scotland. WC-004.

A CORNER OF THE CELLAR AT HAYDON SQUARE, L. & N.W. BONDED STORE.

HYDE PARK, LONDON.
ASK FOR TICKETS VIA CARLISLE & L. & N.W. RAILWAY.

POST CARD
London & North Western Railway.
(FOR ADDRESS ONLY.)
REFERENCES.
Our   Your
DEPT.
STATION.
I beg to acknowledge receipt of your communication dated
and to inform you that the subject of it shall have attention.
Yours truly,
190

Buy the L. & N. W. Series of Pictorial Postcards. 2d. per set of six different cards. Over 5 millions sold.

POST CARD
Caledonian and
London and North Western Railways.
(FOR ADDRESS ONLY.)
Dear
Yours faithfully,
Ask for tickets by the West Coast Royal Mail Route via Carlisle.

Travel to England by the West Coast Royal Mail Route via Carlisle.

The much admired St. Pancras station, together with the Midland Grand Hotel, could be seen as the jewel in the Midland crown and the buildings feature on many postcards. How could you possibly resist the chance to eat lunch to the accompaniment of Herr Drescher's Famous Viennese Orchestra? This delightful poster reproduction dates from 1905 or 1906 and includes a new telephone number and exchange. Note that you could arrive at the hotel by taximeter cab or by tube. MR-209.

2
ST. PANCRAS
Midland
Railway

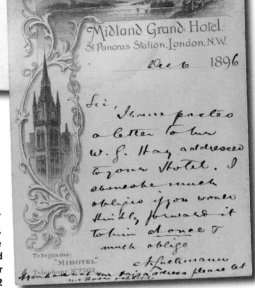

RIGHT: Posted in December 1896, this is the second earliest recorded use of a card classified as a railway official. It is of the smaller court card size and has an undivided back clearly marked 'The address only to be written this side'. The small pictures allowed space for a message on the front. The unanswered question is why the company used a view of Derwentwater in the Lake District, an area they did not serve, to advertise this London hotel. Note the telephone number with no exchange. MR-228.

ABOVE: Another card advertising the Midland Grand Hotel, one of a slightly later series with the earliest recorded use in July 1900. The phone now has an exchange added and the first digit has been dropped. At this date the number was always put before the exchange. MR-222

BELOW: This anonymous uncaptioned view probably dates from around 1908, with a motor car or taxi just visible by the station entrance under the clock tower. Much detail is shown of the splendid entrance to the Midland Grand Hotel, which after many years of neglect, is now restored to its former glory as the St. Pancras Renaissance Hotel, courtesy of the station's new role as the UK terminus of the high speed line from France, now dubbed 'HS1'. The wall on Euston Road is covered with advertising but the hotel is unsullied.

Originally produced by the company in 1904 for their own use, demand from the public persuaded the Midland Railway to issue four sets of six coloured cards in the summer of 1905, including this fine view captioning it as *'The largest single span Passenger Station roof in the world'*. MR-021.

'Going North for the Holidays from St. Pancras Station, Midland Railway'. The original poster, by artist Fred Taylor, was bounded by a maroon frame with 'Going North?' above and 'St. Pancras' below the picture. This busy scene was one of the earliest of this artist's many railway posters and a version of it can be seen displayed at West Kensington, on page 174. The copy shown here was overprinted on the reverse for use by the District Passenger Agent's Office and was sent to a lady in Luton. The machine cancellation postmark has rendered the reverse unsuitable for reproduction here but it appears to refer to a consignment of apples, whilst the printed message stated *'please present this card to the Station Master at ... [filled in as Luton] to whom I have given the necessary instructions'*. The card was published in 1910, this overprinted version being used in October 1914. MR-201.

RIGHT: The Photochrom Company of London published several views of St. Pancras including the busy circa 1904 scene we see here. It certainly looks as though an express is due in if the long line of horse-drawn cabs is anything to go by. The photographer, who can be identified by the initials 'CN' as Photochrom 'staffer' Carl Norman, must have been up some sort of steps, possibly a step-ladder that would normally have been used to service the lights. A porter is keeping a close eye on proceedings and note the boarded platform surfaces.

LEFT: A view across to the bookstall from the cab road at St. Pancras, which includes a number of official looking bowler hatted gentlemen, while a horse stands patiently in front, perhaps awaiting a carriage being transported on a train. This is a Kingsway Series card, a series that were published by W.H. Smith & Son Ltd, this one being posted in April 1912.

ST PANCRAS STATION INTERIOR, MIDLAND RAILWAY.

LEFT: W.H. Smith have included a close-up of their bookstall in this second Kingsway Series card and have two of the bowler hats moved across to feature in the picture as well? Although this appears to be the western extremity of the station, the platform shown is actually No. 2. Platform 1, used only for shorter local trains, was situated in the left distance, towards the outer end of the station. There were seven platforms in all, which remained unchanged until the new arrangements to accommodate international travel via the Channel Tunnel.

DEPARTURE PLATFORM, ST. PANCRAS STATION MIDLAND RAILWAY.

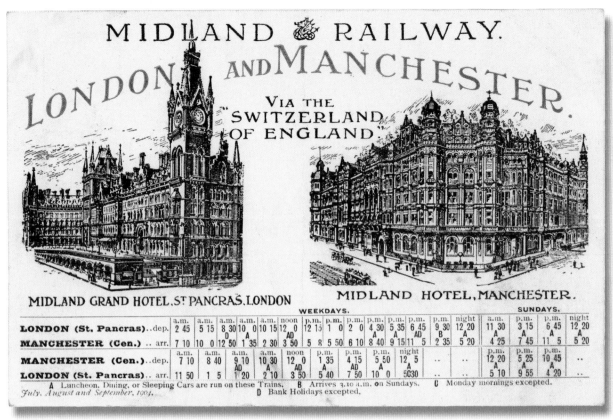

Printed for use by the District Superintendent's Office, this card looks as though it may have been reproduced from a poster. It was probably aimed at the business traveller and shows the trains between St. Pancras and Manchester for July to September 1904. MR-217.

The 4.00pm Bradford and Leeds express pictured just starting away from St. Pancras on an anonymous card of 1907 or 1908. The puff of steam under the front driving wheel of Midland Railway Class '3' 4-4-0 No. 709 tells us that sand is being ejected on to the rails to help the engine pull away without wheel slip. Built in 1901 as No. 804, it became No. 709 under the 1907 renumbering scheme, was rebuilt in 1914 and withdrawn from service in August 1928.

A fine coloured view of an express departing from St. Pancras and about to pass the gas holders that for so many years dominated the line here. Note again that both engines are applying sand to the rails. The Midland Railway had a 'small engine' policy with the result that, as new heavier carriages were introduced, it was not unusual for two engines to be used. The pilot engine, No. 672, was one of the Midland's 'Spinners', graceful single driver locomotives. Built in 1897 and rebuilt in 1909, withdrawal came in September 1926. The train engine, No. 559, was built in 1901 as No. 2597 and is seen here as rebuilt in 1906 and probably shortly after the 1907 renumbering. Substantially rebuilt to '483' Class in 1914, the engine survived until December 1957. The last remaining of these iconic gas holders, No's 8, 10, 11 and 12, were finally decommissioned in 2000 and dismantled a decade or so later, as they were in the way of the new high speed line from the Channel Tunnel. The parts were taken away for refurbishment and No. 8 gas holder has now been re-erected on a nearby site named Gasholder Park, whilst the frames of the other three have been used to enclose new gas holder-shaped blocks of apartments.

Interaction between railways and the public was by no means restricted to stations, as a careful look at this picture shows. Looking south down Regent Street there is little to see at first glance that is railway related but on the right can be seen one of the MR offices, a 'Receiving & Booking Office for Passengers, Parcels & Goods', while waiting outside is a covered dray lettered 'MIDLAND RAILWAY COLLECTING VAN FOR GOODS & PARCELS', which would transport parcels to St. Pancras, as would the 4-wheeled horse-drawn van behind, which is also an MR vehicle. The card is No. 138 in the LL series dating from circa 1904, with just one motor vehicle to be seen, registration No. A306 and possibly a fourth digit. The number of horses on the streets at this period brought its own particular problem, here being dealt with by the two men

138 LONDON. — Oxford Circus — LL.

in white jackets in the centre of the picture. Collected and transported to various of the goods depots, it would then provide another source of traffic for the railway companies, being carried back out to country stations for use as a fertiliser. Note, top left, that the original glass plate negative had been cracked.

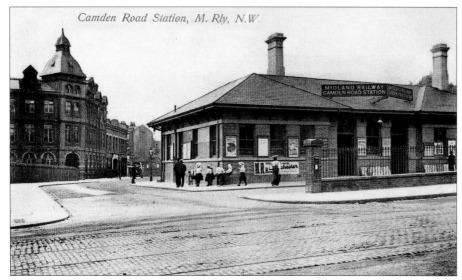

Camden Road Station, M. Rly, N.W.

LEFT: Camden Road station opened on 13th July 1868 and closed during the Great War, on 1st January 1916 but unlike some stations closed during the conflict, it did not reopen. It was situated at the north end of Camden Road tunnel, south of Kentish Town station on the main line. This view, looking across Camden Road to Sandall Road, was captured on a Charles Martin card of circa 1905. Partly hidden behind the lady is a poster for the New Midland Hotel in Manchester, which had opened in September 1903.

RIGHT: Another station that has vanished, on the Tottenham & Hampstead Junction Railway, was that at Junction Road. Opened on 1st January 1872 as Junction Road for Tufnell Park, the name was changed on 1st July 1903. However, this card by E.J. & H. Clarke dates from circa 1913 and still shows the original name displayed on the station. The signal indicates that the approaching train will be taking the Kentish Town line. Although the last train to call was in 1943, official closure was not until 7th June 1949. The station had at one time been very busy but suffered badly from competition when Tufnell Park tube station opened nearby. Station Road remains today as a reminder of its existence.

1863. Junction Road Station, Holloway. E.J.&H.Clarke, E.Finchley

MIDLAND LINE TRAIN.
Engine. No. 39, "Forest Gate."

LEFT: The station at Hornsey Road on the T&HJR opened on 1st January 1872; from 1st February 1882 to 1st July 1903 it was known as Hornsey Road for Hornsey Rise and it closed on 3rd May 1943. On the right are the backs of terrace houses on Fairbridge Road. Heading for Southend, this train will have started from St. Pancras. Taken by Dr Budden in 1898 and published circa 1906 – No. 2087 in the *Locomotive Magazine Series* – the lamps on the front of the engine are in the pre-1902 position, after which the Midland adopted the new standard set of headcodes. The locomotive is London, Tilbury & Southend Railway '37' Class 4-4-2T No. 39 *Forest Gate*, built in 1897, rebuilt in 1907 and withdrawn in 1951. The T&HJR had originally opened in 1868 and represented an attempt by the Great Eastern Railway to establish a terminus in the West End. Closed and abandoned in Janaury 1870, it was then reopened later that year by the Midland who built a connecting line to it from Kentish Town.

Further east on the T&HJR line was St. Ann's Road station, the entrance to which actually faced on to Seven Sisters Road. St. Ann's Road crossed Seven Sisters Road just through the bridge span but the name was chosen because it would not have made sense naming the station Seven Sisters, due to the considerable length of that road. Published by Geo. Saffra of Tottenham, there are no good clues as to the date, the best estimate being circa 1910. The station, opened on 2nd October 1882, was a Second World War closure on 9th August 1942 and did not reopen. The building, a newsagents until 2012, has now been demolished and the site, probably too small for any development, is overgrown and fenced off. The view is looking north, with Metropolitan Electric Tramways

ST ANN'S STATION, SEVEN SISTERS ROAD. Geo Saffra. Publisher, Tottenham

car No. 241 on the right heading south to Finsbury Park. Note, too, that the tobacconists in the building immediately to the left of the station housed a District Office (one of around seventy) for the Tyne Main Coal Co. Ltd of London, so you could order a coal delivery whilst purchasing your pipe tobacco.

Highgate Road, N. W.

There is again more to this picture than is immediately apparent. In the foreground is a passing loop on the tram track and a large scale map of the period shows another loop beyond the bridge, with others onwards at frequent intervals, the trams still being horse-drawn at this time. In the centre is Highgate Road station, which was on two levels, the high level platforms running across the bridge, whilst the low lines were on the left below the level of the road. On the right, immediately before the overbridge, the parapet of the bridge over the low level line can just be seen. The High Level station, on the Tottenham & Hampstead Junction Railway and the last station before the line ended at Gospel Oak, a short distance west, closed in 1915. Three years later, the low level platforms, which lay on the Midland line between the T&HJR and the main line at Kentish Town, also closed. All of the platforms have been demolished and the high level bridge has been reduced to what was the central span, the outer platform spans having been taken away. The card was another in the extensive series of London views published by Charles Martin (of which we shall see many more) and dates from circa 1905.

Published by E. Pouteau, a northbound express is seen passing through West Hampstead station whilst the widening work of 1905-6 was in progress, increasing the four lines to six, with the two lines on the right remaining for goods use. Note the framework for the new booking office. The station was opened by the MR as West End for Kilburn & Hampstead and was changed to plain West End from 1st July 1903 but this lasted only to 1st April 1904 when it became West End & Brondesbury. The staff must have started to wonder where they were working, the name being changed again on 1st September 1905, becoming West Hampstead. This at least lasted until 25th September 1950 when Midland was added and finally, on 16th May 1988, it became West Hampstead Thameslink. The station now has a new entrance on Iverson Road and a new footbridge complete with lifts. It is regarded as an interchange point with the adjacent stations on the Jubilee and London Overground lines and is served by the Bedford-Brighton service in addition to the traditional all stations locals.

Another Pouteau card showing a southbound goods approaching West Hampstead on the goods lines. This is about the same date as the previous picture as the engine is still carrying the earlier pre-1907 livery and there is evidence of construction work on the left and on the platform on the right. Note the signal in the right foreground, with the Midland style roundel on both the Home and Distant arms, rather than the more widely used white bar and black chevron respectively. When W.C. Acfield became MR Signal Superintendent in 1906, he instigated a programme of replacing the roundels to match other railways but it took several years before the task was completed.

Dudding Hill Station. Midland Railway.

B. M. Series.

The railway from Brent to Acton Wells was originally opened as a goods line in 1868. Known as the Midland & South Western Junction Railway (no relation to the railway company of the same name that operated between Cheltenham in Gloucestershire and Southampton), it was worked by the Midland Railway from the outset and was absorbed by that company in 1874. Passenger services were introduced and the station at Dudding Hill opened on 3rd August 1875 but the trains were not well used. The station closed for about five years from 1889 to 1st March 1893 and services then struggled on for a few more years – the MR time table at the end of the 19th century shows the line as part of a service from Moorgate to Mansion House, although they do not look to have been through trains. The passenger service finally ceased on 1st October 1902 and the station was thus already shut at the time of this circa 1905 Reeves Series view, which shows well the rural nature of the area, with Gladstone Park – still there today – beyond the railway. Note the coal wagons in the yard, five of which are private owners belonging to E. Beckett & Co. Ltd of 1 High Road, Willesden, and which from their paintwork look quite new. Despite the early closure of the line to passenger traffic, the yard continued in use until 1964, smokeless zones and a consequent drop in coal traffic no doubt hastening the end. Freight does, however, continue to pass through on a regular basis, the line having been used since 1902 for the purpose which it was originally built. The old station building has gone and the land in the foreground is now all developed – no longer a playground for the children seen watching the camera here. The circular fence surrounds a shaft which is marked on early OS maps but with no description as to its nature.

A second view of the station, which was situated on the east side of Dudding Hill Lane, with access via the steps seen on the left. Posted in 1910, this card in the Sims's Series is looking north and shows Normandy Road to the left with Lancaster Road on the right. With their respective terraces, both had been built since the previous picture.

LEFT: Posted in August 1905, this distressed but rare anonymous view is captioned Harlesden station, which was south of Dudding Hill and had the same opening and closing dates but the name was subject to many changes. It opened as Harrow Road for Stonebridge Park & Willesden but then, on 1st February 1876, Willesden was changed to Harlesden. It became plain Harrow Road from 1st May 1878, with 'for Stonebridge Park and Harlesden' being added on 1st October 1879. On 1st July 1884, it became Stonebridge Park for West Willesden and Harlesden, and finally, on 1st February 1901 the name changed to Harlesden for West Willesden & Stonebridge Park. Although always seeing more travellers than Dudding Hill, it was still not enough to save the line and closure on 1st October 1902 was inevitable, the picture showing the station in use as goods offices subsequently.

RIGHT: For this final look at the Midland Railway we head to the City of London, just in time to spot a well loaded dray heading towards Princes Street and no doubt on up Moorgate, City Road and Pentonville Road to reach St. Pancras. The lettering on the dray shows that it operated between St. Pancras & Castle & Falcon; the latter was probably the name of a one time coaching inn, as many of these continued to be related to travel and became parcels offices. There was a Castle & Falcon at 5 Aldersgate Street from 1684 to 1901, which may have been the origin of the name. The loading of these drays was clearly a skilled job and the two horses had a fair weight to haul up the slopes towards their destination. The Bank of England behind may look a bit odd but it was another thirty years before the upper floors were constructed. This Woodbury Series card was posted on 29th August 1906, although the picture was probably taken three or four years earlier.

3
KING'S
CROSS
Great
Northern
Railway

Opened in 1854, the Great Northern Hotel at King's Cross continued in use as a railway hotel until 1984. It still operates today and is connected directly to the extended station concourse. The ground floor level has been modernised since this picture was taken but in general terms remains instantly recognisable and is now run by one of the large hotel chains. On the left is St. Pancras, also instantly recognisable, although the old beer cellars seen at road level have changed their use. The view up Pancras Road has changed and just beyond the tram you would now see the modern extension to St. Pancras station. This is one of the excellent photographic cards in the Bell Series published by John Walker and was posted in October 1905.

The frontage of the 1852 station at King's Cross had become very cluttered over the years and it was not possible to appreciate the fine design we see here. Fortunately, recent work has seen the area cleared and the building cleaned, once again a sight to behold. The railings below that amazing lamp standard in the right foreground may well be protecting a ventilation opening above the pedestrian subway leading from the main line station to the Metropolitan platforms, which at the time were located to the east of the present station. The widened line platforms here became the Thameslink station until the new passenger facility under St. Pancras was opened. The card is No. 2027 in the Bell series.

ABOVE: A splendid circa 1900 view of King's Cross with no underground station and a horse-drawn tram. There are plenty of GNR displays and even at this date it can be seen that the forecourt was more than a little cluttered. This is another Carl Norman photograph published by Photochrom circa 1905.

BELOW: After the arrival of the tube, the City & South London Railway had entrances both sides of the road while on the far right it is just possible to make out the entrance to the Great Northern, Piccadilly & Brompton Railway; nowadays these are the Northern and Piccadilly lines. Note that 'UNDER GROUND' is two words with no use yet of the larger first and last letters. Only identified by the initials LL, this is another card by French publisher Levy, circa 1907.

RIGHT: An attractive coloured view from the Raphael Tuck & Sons 'London Railway Stations' series, No. 9279, this is looking from the footbridge to the buffer stops down the main departure platform. Styled on the reverse of their cards as 'Art Publishers to their Majesties the King and Queen' and complete with a Royal 'By appointment' crest, Tuck's named these art cards 'Oilettes', as shown in the bottom right corner. They registered the name as a trademark, along with their pallette and easel mark which appears just beneath.

KING'S CROSS STATION. G.N.R.

KING'S CROSS STATION.
The London Terminus of the East Coast Route, the Shortest and Quickest between England and Scotland.

LEFT: Looking in the opposite direction up Platform 1, this card is from a set of six issued under the 'East Coast Route. Shortest and Quickest, England and Scotland' banner. This was the joint operation of Anglo-Scottish expresses by three companies, the Great Northern, North Eastern and North British railways, which were running in competition with the L&NWR and Caledonian Railway's West Coast Joint service from Euston. EC-004

LEFT: Ready to depart from King's Cross, this F. Moore painting has a local train on the left and an express in Platform 1 on the right. The individual locomotives have not been identified beyond being a 4-4-0 on the local and a large boilered 'Atlantic' in charge of the express.

King's Cross Station. G.N.R.

LEFT: From the Locomotive Publishing Company's 'Locomotive Magazine' Series, this picture has been skilfully rendered to represent an after dark departure. The locomotive is one of the Stirling 'Singles', No. 221 and is before June 1899, when it was fitted with an Ivatt domed boiler. It reverted to a domeless boiler in June 1907 and was withdrawn from service in August 1909. The card dates from 1904.

BELOW: By the time Gordon Tidey took this picture, the Stirling singles would have been a rare sight on expresses. However, this is a special for the Wilson Line, heading for one of the north east ports, Hull or Newcastle. It was not unusual for such trains to be put in the hands of an engine that had been retired from top link express work but was still quite capable of handling what was a fairly light load. No. 1004 had a short life, built in January 1895 and withdrawn in August 1914. A member of the 'A1' Class which comprised six engines, these were the last GNR 'Singles' to be built.

SUBURBAN TRAIN, GREAT NORTHERN RAILWAY.

RIGHT: This card was provided for use by the GNR by the LPC and is another F. Moore painting. Built in October 1904, No. 117 was one of a class of heavy tank engines designed to cope with the increasing suburban traffic. Unfortunately, it was found that they were too heavy to work on the Metropolitan, so with condensers removed they were sent out to the Nottingham and West Riding areas for goods work instead. No. 117 was withdrawn from service in April 1933. This is one of several LPC cards that were overprinted on the reverse for the GNR, having 'Great Northern Railway' in old English-style lettering printed at the top of the correspondence space. GN-043.

Photographed at the same spot as the previous picture, with the corner of Belle Isle signal box just showing on the left, 'B3' Class 'Single' No. 879 heads up the bank to Holloway. Built in 1894, the engine was scrapped in January 1911. Beyond the signals on the right, a saddle tank can be seen shunting in King's Cross goods yard and on the left, through the arches of York Road Bridge, it is just possible to see a bit of the motive power depot. This whole area beyond the main line has been extensively redeveloped since the end of steam and the Channel Tunnel rail link now runs across the site too.

We are in the bounds of the Great Northern's King's Cross shed, with a GNR saddle tank and wagons but the roundhouse itself was of Midland Railway origin. It dated from 1859, in the era before St. Pancras station had been built and Midland trains used King's Cross, arriving via Bedford and Hitchin. The Midland's shed on their own line at Kentish Town opened in 1868-9, trains having started using St. Pancras in August 1868 and the roundhouse, which was unsurprisingly known as 'the Derby shed', was then handed over to the Great Northern, who used it mostly to house goods and tank engines. It was demolished during an L&NER programme to improve the facilities at King's Cross shed in 1931-2.

LEFT: This picture was posed during a visit to the shed in 1919, with two youthful engine cleaners sitting on the cab roof of 0-6-0ST No. 1212 which dated from June 1897. With this example being rebuilt in October 1925 and lasting in service until October 1954, these saddle tanks were useful engines. Looking at the generally murky atmosphere one can sympathise with the cleaners! Space was limited and this gives a good idea of the crowded conditions, as well as the skills required to plan having each engine in the right place at the right time. The photographer is anonymous but the card was published in the LPC's 'Locomotive Magazine' Series.

RIGHT: A more open view of King's Cross shed circa 1905, showing a good selection of the express engines of the day. No. 285 on the right is standing under a set of sheerlegs, which could be used to raise one end of the engine for examinations and work to be carried out underneath. It would be possible to take out one of the driving wheel sets for instance, if attention were needed to the bearings. In the gloom behind the straight road shed, part of the original curved fronted locomotive shed of 1851 can just be made out, which had been converted for use as a carriage repair works by around 1870.

LEFT: Taken by Gordon Tidey, this photograph shows members of The Railway Club on an organised visit to King's Cross shed on 17th April 1920 and it is interesting to note the style of clothing worn for a trip of this sort nearly a hundred years ago. At ground level, the tall gentleman wearing a wing collar shirt, tenth from left, is believed to be J.N. Maskeleyne but he is the only one to be identified so far. The RC members are posed on and around Gresley 'H3' Class 2-cylinder 2-6-0 No. 1655, which was new from Doncaster Works in October 1916 and lasted in service until November 1960.

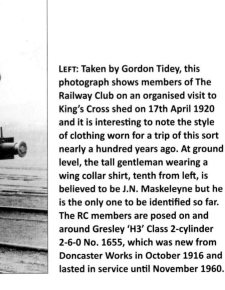

This is Copenhagen Tunnel, which was later to become well known as the location for part of the Ealing Comedy *The Ladykillers*, a 1955 film where bodies were dropped into trains. Mrs Wilberforce's house was located approximately where the wall can be seen below the building top right. Here, we see Ivatt 4-4-2T No. 1531 passing Copenhagen Junction signal box as it heads to Moorgate. This 'C2' Class engine (L&NER Class 'C12') was built in December 1903 and was fitted with a condenser for working through the tunnels to Moorgate. This was designed to cut the amount of steam fouling the atmosphere, not, as someone once suggested, to make the engine smaller to fit in the tunnel! There was a sign at Barbican station 'Engines must condense' still to be seen after steam workings had ceased. No. 1531 became L&NER No. 4531 in August 1925 and No. 7384 in October 1946. Renumbered by British Railways in October 1948 as No. 67384, withdrawal took place in May 1956. The arrival of the larger Gresley tank locomotives had displaced these 'C2' engines and they spent much of there later life on branch line and other lighter services. Beyond the wall top right was Caledonian Road coal and goods depot, a small local yard which was served directly from the giant King's Cross goods depot via a single line rising up just out of sight to the left of the tunnel. This whole area is the subject of a wonderfully detailed working 2mm finescale model, the work of the London-based The Model Railway Club, which has so far taken over three decades to construct and is still some way from completion. Whilst one or two liberties have, by necessity, been taken with certain aspects of the local geography, the railway is accurately modelled and the effect is quite spectacular. Those who don't know the layout are recommended to search out the videos of it on YouTube.

RIGHT: When Holloway station was opened on 1st August 1856 it had only a single island platform. At an unknown date between 1871 and 1894, a second platform was added but it was not aligned with the original. This new platform, designated 'Down', straddled the bridge carrying the line over Holloway Road. Subsequently, a new platform was constructed which was aligned with the original and it is surmised that this, with its improved accommodation, came into use on 6th May 1901, when the station was renamed Holloway & Caledonian Road. Stirling 'Single' No. 666 was new in November 1881 and was withdrawn in October 1906. The picture, which is the work of Dr Tice F. Budden, is noted as being a Scotch Express and was taken circa 1900, there being no sign yet of the new platform on the right. The site of the sidings is now covered by a residential development.

LEFT: The photographer, Bernard Wren Groom, was here standing on the new platform at what was now Holloway & Caledonian Road station. It is one of several pictures taken here and published by this young man from Cambridge. Large 'Atlantic' No. 1414 powers north with an unidentified express. Built in March 1906 and superheated in June 1918, No. 1414 probably gained a few extra years of use because of the Second World War, being withdrawn in October 1944. The station suffered badly from competition when the Great Northern, Piccadilly & Brompton tube station, Caledonian Road, was opened literally next door to the main line establishment, such that it was closed on 1st October 1915. It had been demolished and the platforms cleared away by the mid 1920s. The large structure on the left was part of a brush works.

RIGHT: Harringay was not one of the original stations on the Great Northern main line. The construction of it was in connection with the British Land Company and their development of the site of the one time Harringay House. From 18th June 1951, West was added to the name but this was dropped from 27th May 1971, the station becoming plain Harringay again. This view is looking north and visible through the span holding the main building is Harringay Engine Viaduct, provided in 1893 and replaced in 1961. The booking office was destroyed by fire on 17th April 1968. The anonymous card has the date 24th June 1905 written on the back, which could well be when the picture was taken.

The photographer of this view would have been standing at the south end of Hornsey station with the signal box just behind him. The view gives a feeling for the vast sweep of Ferme Park sidings, with the Up yard on the left and the Down sidings on the right. At its greatest extent and its widest point, including the running lines, there were sixty tracks. There are also some spectacular looking signals, very tall, and note the spectacles lower down the posts where the lamps would have been placed, as well as the attendant substantial staying posts. Meanwhile, the locomotive in the centre of the picture is not Great Northern but an interloper from the North Eastern Railway, whose engines were not normally seen in the south. No. 1875 had come up to King's Cross on one of two troop specials taking volunteers from Harrogate on their way to Aldershot. The trains had arrived in London at 1.05am and 4.14am on the morning of Sunday 3rd June 1900, so this picture has perhaps caught one of the engines heading for home. No. 1875 was a 'Q' Class 4-4-0 of 1896, superheater fitted in 1915 and withdrawn in October 1931. The second train was hauled by No. 491, a '59' Class 0-6-0. The two signal boxes on view here are Ferme Park Up Goods and Ferme Park Down Goods and the north end of Harringay Engine Viaduct can just be made out in the distance beyond and to the right of No. 1875's tender. The card was published in early 1905, 'Locomotive Magazine Series' No. 1203. The higher land in the right background was known as the Hog's Back.

Looking north from the Hog's Back circa 1910, towards Hornsey station in the left centre distance, with the expanse of the Down yard sidings in the foreground and the Up yard over on the far right. An Ivatt 'Atlantic' heads towards King's Cross with an Up express, whilst an 0-6-0ST drifts light engine down the north ramp of Harringay Engine Viaduct. This bridge, built mainly to facilitate access to and between the Up and Down goods yards without blocking the main lines and for light engine movements between the sidings, is still in use in its rebuilt form today. There are also still yards here on both sides of the line, that on the Up side now housing Hornsey Thameslink Depot, opened in 2016 and partly on the site of the steam shed just visible here in the right middle distance. The tall chimney on the left belonged to Hornsey Borough Electricity Works, which received coal deliveries by rail, and beyond it on the skyline the dome of Alexandra Palace can just be made out.

A close-up of the northern end of the ramp down from Harringay Engine Viaduct, looking southwards in a photograph taken in 1907 by F.E. Mackay and published by E. Pouteau. On the right is the Down yard, with Hog's Back Hill behind, from which the previous picture was taken. Note that there are three staying posts in view from which cables run to the ground and to the signal gantry, in order to support it in high winds; a fourth post is almost certainly out of sight on the left. The yards here were used for sorting coal wagons, these being some of the sidings for returning empties.

Also taken in 1907 by F.E. Mackay and published by Pouteau was this driver's eye view of loaded wagons being shunted at the south end of what was termed No. 3 coal sidings. Ahead, the shunters stand with their coupling poles awaiting the arrival of the wagon and note the scissors crossover on the left.

RIGHT: The coal stage at Hornsey shed is just visible in the previous picture, above the steam from the 0-6-0ST descending the ramp from the viaduct. Here we get a close-up view of it following a bit of a mishap. Clearly the driver shunting coal wagons had misjudged the distance, with the result that one wagon came through the end wall, most of which seems to have finished on the path by the New River. The shed roof can be seen over the two men pointing and discussing the problem, whilst those on the path have seen the photographer and stopped work while the picture is taken. The date was 14th June 1907 and the card, by the Hampden Photo-Printing Co. of Hornsey, probably came out the same day. Hornsey shed had been desperately needed to ease the situation at King's Cross and came into use in late 1899.

BELOW: Hornsey station opened on 7th August 1850, when the line from Peterborough to the temporary terminus at Maiden Lane was brought in to use, four years before the line reached King's Cross. This early view by Dr Budden is before the Down platform (on the right) was made into an island, work probably carried out following the similar changes at Harringay in 1900. For many years there was a turntable beyond the wall on the right, which was removed circa 1930. Three trains feature in this busy scene with the rear of a departing Up service on the left. In the centre a northbound express is hauled by No. 774, built in December 1885 and withdrawn in January 1905. The tank engine on the local train had a longer life; a member of the 'G3' Class of 0-4-4Ts, No. 695 was built in March 1884, fitted with a domed boiler in January 1912 and was withdrawn in April 1926. It was equipped with condensing gear and cut down boiler mountings for working on the Metropolitan. Faint in the background are the very tall signals seen on page 41.

Curious mishap at Hornsey, G.N.R.

LEFT: A Class 'G1' 0-4-4T stars in another picture at Hornsey by Dr Budden, again dating from before the conversion of the Down platform to an island and on another 'Locomotive Magazine Series' card from circa 1905. The condensing gear on No. 940 is clear to see, as is the birdcage guard's lookout on the front carriage. This was part of a set of close-coupled, 4-wheeled coaches, which were built in quantity for suburban services. The board on the locomotive's smokebox door indicates this as a GN Main Line stopping service, which would no doubt have been expected to keep to a smart time table even allowing for the four tracks. Completed in June 1893, No. 940 was fitted with a domed boiler in 1913 and withdrawn from service in 1924. The platforms, once increased to four both here and at Harringay, have now been reduced to two at both places, just serving the slow lines.

Stroud Green Station   Stapleton Hall Road   N.

The High Barnet Branch left the GNR main line just north of Finsbury Park station and the first stop on it was at Stroud Green. The line was opened in 1867 but the station here was not added until 1881, probably accounting for the way it had to be squeezed in utilising the bridge. Here in this view from circa 1904 we are looking southwards on Stapleton Hall Road, with the station entrance to the right. The nameboard above the bridge gives a clue to the fact that the platforms run across the bridge and the ends of two shelters on the nearer (Up) platform can be seen. There was clearly competition for coal sales here, with several merchants having offices on the left and another opposite. The odd little shack with corrugated roof and cupola in front of the coal merchants was a fire station, which was no longer shown on a map of 1914; part of the wheels and the top of an extending ladder can be seen just behind it. There is also that other favourite to be found outside stations – an auctioneers office, in this case belonging to the firm of Gilbert & How. Hidden away is the line of the Tottenham & Hampstead Joint Railway, which actually crosses diagonally through the centre of this view but is below road level. Stroud Green station buildings suffered from a fire in 1967 and were then demolished. The building on the right was apparently the station masters house, where presumably he occupied the two floors above road level. Stroud Green station buildings suffered from a fire in 1967 and were then demolished. The building on the right was apparently the station masters house, where presumably he occupied the two floors above Newton Chambers premises, and this building survives, as does the bridge, now carrying the Parkland Walk cycleway and footpath along the old trackbed. The card is by Charles Martin.

Stroud Green Station. G. N. Ry.

LEFT: Stroud Green station at platform level, with the two shelters on the Up platform in view on another Charles Martin card. The destination board on the front of the engine just arriving on a Down local is unclear but probably read Alexandra Palace. The engine is 'C2' Class 4-4-2T No. 1533, built in December 1903. Fitted with a condenser for Moorgate trains, this was removed in 1922, by which time more powerful Gresley Class 'N2' 0-6-2Ts had displaced these Ivatt engines from the London Area. No. 1533 was sent to Grantham and withdrawn in December 1937. Many remained in service for a good time, as they were suited to branch line work in the country and the last of the class survived in use until December 1958.

RIGHT: Setting off from Broad Street in the City, the North London Railway also had trains heading up the High Barnet Branch, in this case to then turn towards Muswell Hill station on the Alexandra Palace Branch. Built in 1898, 4-4-0T No. 88 was probably fairly new when this picture was taken, once again by Dr Budden. This is an excellent view of a standard NLR passenger train, with ten 4-wheeled coaches sandwiched between two brake vans with birdcage lookouts. No. 88 was withdrawn in November 1928 and the card was published in 1905, 'Locomotive Magazine Series' No. 1431. Note, too, the lattice-posted somersault signal.

Crouch End Station N. from Hornsey Lane.

RIGHT: Looking from Hornsey Lane, with Hornsey Rise just coming in on the right, this is a very countrified view of Crouch End station. Opened on 22nd August 1867, the station closed with the rest of the branch on 5th July 1954, when the new Northern Line services started running, although the line had suffered a temporary closure prior to this, from 29th October 1951 to 7th January 1952 as a coal saving measure. The work of Charles Martin, the card was posted in July 1907.

A good overall view of the platforms at Crouch End, again by Charles Martin. Passengers can be seen waiting for an Up train, whilst in the foreground a permanent way gang are at work on the Up line. On the left edge of the picture, a wagon probably loaded with coal, stands at the end of the single siding provided here for such traffic. The card again dates from circa 1905.

Crouch End Station.

No. 464.   HIGHGATE STATION.

Highgate station also opened on 22nd August 1867 and closed on 5th July 1954. The Underground station had opened in 1940 and the line from Finsbury Park to Highgate only survived until withdrawal of the very limited service to Alexandra Palace. The island platform was not original, the station as built having just the two outer platforms with a line for the reversal of trains in the centre. Surprisingly, the site has not been cleared since closure but the Northern Line station is at a lower level and this, together with access ways, probably precludes any new works. All the staff in view pose for the photographer, probably Gordon Smith, who published the card circa 1905. Note the decorative Imperial Property Investment Co. hut in the background.

With this final view of the station at Highgate, this is as far as we go out on the Great Northern Railway. Situated in a deep cutting between two sets of tunnels, here we see the portals at the north end, along with a rather neat set of somersault signals, set on very short lattice posts and against a white-washed background to aid sighting. This is looking in the Down direction, with the Distant signals being for Park Junction where the Alexandra Palace Branch turned off to the right just beyond the tunnel. The names of the two who feature here have been appended to the reverse of the card, with the man on the left stated to be one R. Young, whilst the station master is F.M. Wynne. The card, dating from 1904-5, is by E.F. Clarke; note his surname is upside down in the bottom right corner of the card, which was usual for this publisher.

The terminus at Broad Street was opened by the North London Railway on 1st November 1865. It had been financed to a considerable extent by the L&NWR, who owned and operated the goods station at ground level, which was accessed by means of hydraulically operated wagon lifts. The line was built from Dalston mainly on a viaduct, which kept the amount of land required and housing to be demolished to

Broad Street Station   London

4
BROAD STREET
North London Railway

a minimum. In 1902 during the morning rush hour, trains were arriving at or departing from one of Broad Street's eight platforms at the rate of more than one a minute, being used by over 27 million passengers that year but the competition from the electric trams, and then buses and the Underground, caused a dramatic decline from that high point over the following decades. The station and the line from Dalston Junction finally closed on 30th June 1986, when the remaining services were diverted to Liverpool Street. This early view was posted on 30th March 1901 to a *Mademoiselle* in Paris. Horse-drawn buses and cabs, together with a dray belonging to the GNR, contribute to a busy scene.

A platform view of Broad Street on an early postcard has to date failed to appear, so a view looking out must suffice, albeit one filled with interest. Dating from around 1905, this card was Locomotive Publishing Co. No. 3458. On the left is some smart looking L&NWR stock that would have come in from the Watford direction. Trying to hide behind the water column is NLR 4-4-0T No. 6 of 1894, a renewal of an 1870 engine which was itself renewed in 1909. To the right there is a small coal stage – hand coaling – and two water tanks, alongside which is another 4-4-0T, with a number beginning with 2 and carrying a New Barnet headboard. Right again is Broad Street signal box, which controlled the station approach, including the signals standing tall over all the clutter. On the right is an unidentified L&NWR engine, probably a 2-4-2T. Note the circle and diamond hooked on to its chimney to indicate which route the train was taking. The engine is standing by another small coal stage, every space possible on this limited site being put to use. From a large scale OS, the chimney on the left appears to be on railway land but its role here is otherwise not indicated.

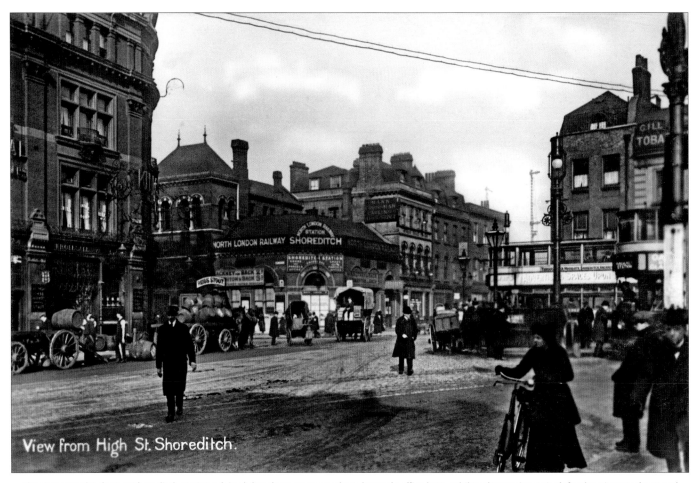

View from High St. Shoreditch.

The sign over the door at Shoreditch station advised that there was a goods and parcels office here, whilst a larger sign to its left advertises Hackney and back 2d or Homerton and back 3d. The line passed through the station at a higher level than the road and it is possible to make out two very tall signals above the tram. The station was situated on the corner of Old Street where it met with Shoreditch High Street, to the left of the photographer, and Midland Road, straight ahead. The station was rebuilt circa 1930 and survives today as the Old Shoreditch Station cafe, whilst the North London Line (re-opened in 2011 as part of the London Overground system) now runs through on its way to Stratford.

RIGHT: This view from around 1904 shows a North London train for Broad Street running in to one of the six platforms at Dalston Junction station. The platforms to the east were served by Broad Street to Poplar trains, whilst the others would have seen NLR services heading for Richmond, as well as L&NWR and Great Northern Railway trains. Services required no less than seven tables in the 1910 *Bradshaw's Rail Times* time table. Opened on 1st November 1865, the station was closed on 30th June 1986 when the last remaining Broad Street services were diverted. However, the recent works that have seen the old East London line extended also saw a new station opened here, on 27th April 2010, albeit the platforms are hidden beneath a new office and retail development.

Dalston Junction. Interior.

One of the more unusual views published by Pouteau was this photograph of Western Junction Dalston signal box in around 1908, showing one of the spritely North London Railway 4-4-0Ts, No. 68, heading for Broad Street with a standard formation local train. Behind the cabin the line reduces from four tracks to two as it heads eastwards, first to pass under Boleyn Road and then through the short tunnel taking the line beneath Kingsland High Street and Ridley Road, and on towards Hackney. Today, between the Boleyn Road bridge and the tunnel is Dalston Kingsland station, opened by British Railways in 1983 and close to the site of Kingsland station, opened in 1850 but closed in 1865 when the NLR extended the line to Broad Street. The signals on view are all worthy of study. The very tall junction signals positioned just the other side of Kingsbury Road bridge were required so that they could be seen over King Henry's Walk bridge (another 100 yards or so west) by the crews of trains departing Mildmay station. Note, too, the sighting boards behind the arms of the signals in the foreground. Today, the box is long gone and the junction no longer exists; the four Broad Street lines have been relaid as two as part of the East London Line to Shoreditch and points south but there is no physical connection with the twin tracks of the North London Line heading to and from Hackney Central.

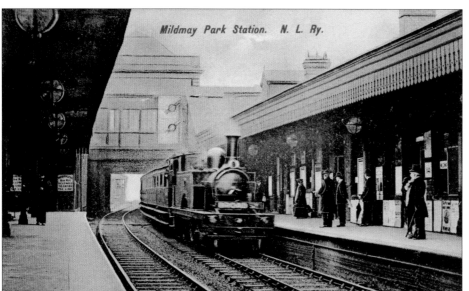

Mildmay Park Station. N. L. Ry.

LEFT: Heading west from Dalston Junction, after only a quarter of a mile we reach the station at Mildmay Park, also seen with a Broad Street train arriving. These little North London tank engines may have been of small stature but they could certainly do what was required of them and continued to handle the lengthy trains required until the mid 1920s. There were four platforms here, that on the left being an island. Opened on 1st January 1880, the station had a shorter life than most on the line and was closed on 1st July 1934. The lines through here have never been straightened, however, and thus still follow the curves of the non-existent platforms.

BELOW LEFT: The London & North Western Railway was closely associated with the North London for many years and finally took over the company in 1922. They ran a 'City to City Express', which comprised one return journey between Birmingham and Broad Street, Mondays to Fridays, with a Breakfast Car in the mornings and a Restaurant Car in the evenings. A special typewriting room was also provided where businessmen could have their correspondence typed for them on the journey. The Birmingham departure was at 8.20am, arriving Broad Street at 10.35am, calling only at Coventry en route. The return departed at 5.25pm and arrived at 7.40pm, with stops at Willesden and Coventry. The express was depicted on a Tuck 'Oilette' card, in their 'Famous Expresses' Series XI. It was shown passing a North London Railway train probably near Mildmay Park and provided a stark contrast between the modern express carriages and those of the local train.

L&NWR. City to City Express Birmingham to Broad Street.

RIGHT AND BELOW: The L&NWR issued this fascinating postcard of the typewriting room on the 'City to City Express' in 1909. We see the young lady typist hard at work in what appears to be a conversion of a standard compartment. LNW-746. (*In a very early nod to equality, another similar card showed that the typist could also be male*)

POST CARD.

A Typewriting Room is provided on the undermentioned trains. Letters, etc., can be typed en route; charges moderate. All matters are dealt with as confidential.

(FOR ADDRESS ONLY.)

Buy the L. & N. W. Series of Pictorial Postcards. 2d. per set of six different cards. Over 9 millions sold.

	a.m.	a.m.
Birmingham (New Street) dep.	†8.20	8.40
Coventry	†8.43	...
London (Broad Street City) arr.	†10.35	...
" (Euston)	...	10.40
	p.m.	p.m.
London (Euston) ... ... dep.	4.45	5.*20
" (Broad Street City) "	...	5.‡25
Coventry ... ... arr.	...	7.†17
Birmingham (New Street) "	6.45	7.†40

† Sats. excepted. * Change at Willesden (Sats. excepted).

L. & N. W. R.

TYPEWRITING ROOM ON BIRMINGHAM-LONDON TRAINS

Canonbury Station. N. L. Ry.

The station here was the second one for Canonbury, opening on 1st December 1870 and replacing the original situated a little to the east, which had been named Newington Road & Balls Pond until just a few months previously. Just arriving is a North London train bound for Kilburn, as indicated by the destination board beneath the smokebox door. These served a useful purpose, as a handy last minute check for passengers, with the number of different destinations that were served. The station is still open but with a small modern entrance and only simple shelters on the four platforms.

Highbury Station. (N. L. Ry.)

Highbury station platforms have also now been provided with new accommodation, the old buildings seen here having been swept away. This could well be regarded as a good thing, as in general the old North London stations had become seriously dilapidated and, indeed, the whole line was included in Beeching's closure proposals. Rarely to be seen in this position are the advertising signs, no doubt vitreous enamel, on the platform faces.

Highbury station exterior was really quite impressive. Opened on 26th September 1850 as Islington, the station had been renamed Islington & Highbury on 1st June 1864, with the present name of Highbury & Islington coming in to use on 1st July 1872 following rebuilding. Note the advertisements, mostly for auctioneers and estate agents. The one to the right, above the head of the man in the foreground, carries the name of Tidey & Son; Robert Tidey's son was H. Gordon Tidey, born in 1879 and listed in the 1811 census as a surveyor and valuer, who is better known today as one of the great railway photographers, with a few of his pictures featuring in these pages. The architect responsible for the design of the six stations built by the NLR in the early 1870s was Edwin Henry Horne, who was forced to retire in 1880 aged just 37 due to ill health. Sadly, this magnificent building had long damaged twice by German bombs in the Second World War. The station is now an interchange between the Victoria Line, London Overground's East London and North London lines, and the older Great Northern & City Railway, and boasts a most unprepossessing, uncompleted entrance. In 2015, a petition to rebuild the 1872 façade seen here was presented to Parliament. The card, published by Bell's of Leigh-on-Sea, was posted to Germany in August 1908, which probably gives a fairly accurate idea of its date.

Barnsbury Station.

LEFT: A number of the stations had to be rebuilt when the line between Camden Town and Dalston Junction was quadrupled in 1871. This included Caledonian Road & Barnsbury station, which was moved slightly to the east. The station had been opened as Barnsbury on 21st November 1870, replacing the original Caledonian Road station of 1852. As a result, the main building was on Roman Way rather than Caledonian Road and the name Barnsbury was included in the façade of the impressive building. Today, there is not even an entrance to the station at this east end. The renaming to Caledonian Road & Barnsbury took place on 22nd May 1893.

Caledonian Road & Barnsbury Station.

LEFT: The North London Railway was always generous with space – very necessary given the volume of passengers carried in the morning and evening rush hours – and here again we see wide platforms as an L&NWR train runs in. There are two signal boxes in view but, by 1915, only the more modern looking box on the right or Up side appeared on maps, so this circa 1904 view seems to have captured modernisation in progress. Also shown are the covered entrances to the steps at the end of the platforms, leading down towards Caledonian Road which was then reached by a footpath. Only the central island platform remains today.

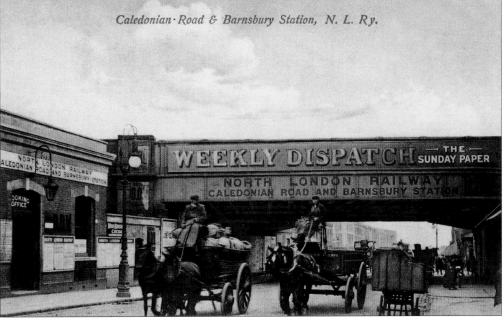

Caledonian-Road & Barnsbury Station, N. L. Ry.

RIGHT: The west entrance carried the full name of Caledonian Road and Barnsbury, and it was also painted on the bridge span. This building has also gone and there is now a pedestrian route to the station on the far side of the bridge. The Weekly Dispatch became the Sunday Dispatch in 1928, continuing under that name until 1961 when it merged with the Sunday Express. Today the bridge span is painted blue and has 'THE CALLY' painted on it in white letters. Note how the wall beneath the span is plastered with advertisements, a common occurrence as we shall see.

Camden Town exterior survives today virtually unchanged, even with the NLR title and the now incorrect station name. The building, one of Horne's designs, is Grade II listed and is the only one of his stations to remain in railway use. It is situated on the corner of Bonny Street and Camden Road, and is the station opened in 1870, when it was resited to the west of the original position. The renaming to Camden Road was to avoid confusion with the underground station of the same name, the change taking place under British Railways on 25th September 1950. Two horse trams

complete a picture which suggests a more leisurely age. As always the trams act as mobile advertisement hoardings, with the names of Milkmaid Milk and Bryant & May prominent here. The inked date mirrored that of the postmark and would again be fairly accurate as regards when the picture was taken.

ABOVE: The line we are following now heads round to the north and then west to reach Hampstead Heath station, which was opened under the auspices of the Hampstead Junction Railway on 2nd January 1860. Situated on the east side of South End Road, the modern entrance and booking office occupies roughly the position of the Goods & Parcels Office on the left here; the old buildings along with the wonderful sign – 'TRAINS TO … SCOTLAND & IRELAND' – have gone. Typically for the period, the wall of the building on the right is covered with advertising – how many people actually looked up there and studied them? Other distractions included a florists shop on right, opposite the station entrance, and a wine merchants just inside.

LEFT: Having passed through the lengthy Hampstead Tunnel (1,167 yards) and Finchley Road & Frognal station, we reach West End Lane. This was opened on 1st March 1888, and served under that name until 5th May 1975, when it became West Hampstead. It is situated on the west side of West End Lane, adjacent to the old Midland Railway station to the north and the Metropolitan station to the south, the three now being seen as an interchange point. A North London train is departing, showing the rear with the birdcage lookout contrasting against the low roofs of the rest of the stock. West End Lane is now the most basic of the three stations that make up this interchange point, with no more than a simple shelter on one platform although the building over the bridge remains. Note over the head of the man bending over a bicycle is another poster that the L&NWR used on a postcard (LNW-743), advertising Manchester in 3 hours 30 minutes with the front of a locomotive.

West End Lane Station.

RIGHT: No. 65, one of the North London Railway 0-6-0Ts, was recorded as being a renewal of an 1888 engine and was built in 1905. The use of 'renewal' was something of a ruse, connected with accounting requirements and capital stock. Heading west, the goods train, the end of which is out of sight, represents a good load for the engine and has just passed through West End Lane station.

The engine was to be one of the last survivors of the class, becoming L&NWR No. 2883 in 1922, LM&SR No. 7513 in June 1927 and renumbered again as No. 27513 in August 1934. Its final number was under British Railways, becoming No. 58854 in June 1950 and the engine was finally withdrawn in November 1956. The photograph by R. Welby King was published by Pouteau circa 1905.

H.R.M. Series, 70.   Kensal Rise Station.

LEFT: The final visit in this direction is to the station at Kensal Rise, where great attention was paid to the photographer. This is the last stop before Willesden Junction, already visited. The station opened as Kensal Green on 1st July 1873, replacing the original 1861 station Kensal Green & Harlesden, which was about a mile towards Willesden Junction. When originally built, Kensal Rise was in fairly open country and served what was described as a National Athletic Ground in nearby Brondesbury Park which, for a time, was home to Queens Park Rangers football club. The area, athletic ground included, is now entirely built-up. The remaining part of the building on the right is still recognisable, albeit much altered, whilst the booking office on the bridge has gone, with a new entrance at platform level. Two interesting sets of wheels to study – a 3-wheeled hand cart and a perambulator that is a real work of art.

Hackney Station, Mare Street.

ABOVE: Hauled by a 'Coal Tank' 0-6-2T and watched by a couple of strollers in the field, a nine-coach rake of L&NWR 6-wheeled stock heads away from Kensal Rise station in 1907. According to the top line of the destination board on the bunker of the engine, the train was bound for Willesden Junction; the second line will start 'via' but is otherwise indecipherable, whilst the bottom line reads 'and Mansion House'. The houses in the right background face on to Purves Road, whilst the field on the left is also now hidden beneath residential streets.

ABOVE: Turning east from Dalston Junction, the first station reached was that at Hackney. The building survives, although no longer in railway use but as a live music venue. A path from Amhurst Road now leads to the new station entrance through the site of the Universal Parcels Office to the right. The 1850 station had originally been on the east side of the bridge, opening in this new position on 1st December 1870. The station was closed on 23rd April 1944 (official date) although the last train was actually on 15th May. Transport developments in London saw the station reopening as Hackney Central on 12th May 1980. Note that every possible space on the supporting walls is earning money from advertising.

LEFT: The L&NWR made quite extensive use of their own postcards in overprinting them with advertising and then adding in red the address of local agents, in this case the office seen above alongside Hackney station. They were presumably for distribution to local businesses that might be persuaded to use their services. LNW overprint W093.

POST CARD

THE L. & N.W.R. SERIES OF PICTORIAL POSTCARDS

Printed in England.

LONDON AND NORTH WESTERN RAILWAY.

"The London and North Western Railway Company's trains are noted for Punctuality, Speed, Smooth Riding, Dustless Tracks, Safety and Comfort, and is the Oldest Established Firm

West Coast Royal Mail Route.

The Premier Route to and from IRELAND, SCOTLAND, WALES, The MIDLANDS and NORTH of ENGLAND.

The Highway to and from Ireland is Via HOLYHEAD.

FIVE Sailings each way daily.

Express Goods Trains daily between LONDON and all Principal Towns.

For Business or Pleasure travel by "NORTHWESTERN."

Breakfast, Luncheon, Dining and Sleeping Cars.

The AGENT at UNIVERSAL PARCELS OFFICE, N. L. Railway, HACKNEY, (Tele. No. 1609 Dalston), will be pleased to supply any information, and make arrangements for your comfortable travel; or for the collection of parcels, luggage and goods.

Goods and Parcels should be carefully consigned per "L. & N. W. RLY."

Church Road, Homerton.

Homerton station opened on 1st October 1868. It was never relocated nor renamed and its closure date was the same as Hackney but its reopening was on 13th May 1985. The typical North London Railway signal box provided here can be seen to the left of the bridge, with two of its front windows wide open, together with a signal almost hidden by the tree. The station is to the right, the frontage to which has four handsome arches and 'NORTH LONDON RAILWAY HOMERTON STATION' on the impediment above. This view, looking south on Church Road, is on yet another of the distinctive Charles Martin postcards, a total of thirteen of which illustrate this chapter alone, this one postally used in January 1906. The Great Northern Railway sign was well placed, drawing attention to their coal depot not far away in Hackney Wick and again there was no shortage of advertising elsewhere on the bridge. Although the station is again in use today, the scene here has much changed, even to the street name, which is now Barnabas Road. The station building and the shop next to it have gone, as has the building on the left, whilst the bridge itself has been completely rebuilt. The raised pavements remain however.

RIGHT: Bow station was opened on 26th September 1850 but the grand building pictured here dates from 1870 and is again the work of E.H. Horne. The ground floor contained a commodious booking office, a waiting room and a refreshment room, whilst upstairs was a large hall which had many uses over the years, from the Salvation Army to billiards and dancing. The hall was demolished following a fire in 1956, while the lower level continued for a few more years as a parcels office, closing in 1965. The site was finally cleared ten years later. The splendid piece of Victoriana is the 30ft high Bryant & May Testimonial Fountain, erected in 1872 and paid for by the employees of the firm to commemorate the defeat of a proposed tax on matches. The fountain was removed for the widening of Bow Road in 1952-3.

LEFT: Unusually for Charles Martin, this view of a train arriving at Bow station has been somewhat retouched possibly because it was still moving when the original photograph was taken and thus was slightly blurred. However, it can just be discerned that this was a service bound for Broad Street, having started from Poplar, although is not possible to identify the engine beyond it being one of the NLR 4-4-0Ts. On the other line, there appears to be the rear of a goods train heading for the docks.

RIGHT: Situated on East India Dock Road, the station at Poplar opened on 1st August 1866. Initially, trains ran through to Blackwall which involved running through (but not stopping at) the Great Eastern Railway's Poplar station. The North London station was known as Poplar (East India Road) but this service ceased in July 1890 and the NLR station then became the terminus for passenger trains from Broad Street. The station was a wartime casualty, closing in May 1944, although the booking office remained open in connection with a substitute bus service that operated for another year. Note here that the trams are picking up current using the conduit system. The Docklands Light Railway's All Saints station now occupies the site and the whole scene has changed. It is just possible to see All Saints church in this Edwardian view published by Stengel.

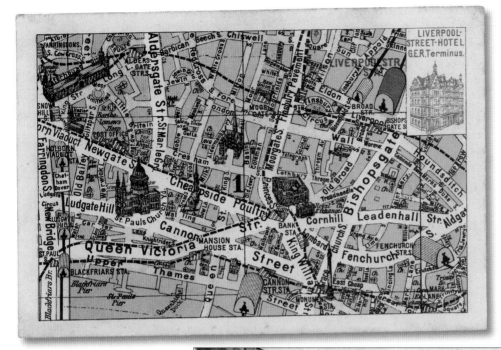

5
LIVERPOOL STREET
Great Eastern Railway

ABOVE: Used in Belgium in 1908, this anonymous map card of the City publicises the Great Eastern Railway's Liverpool Street Hotel. The style of the back of the card suggests an earlier date, perhaps 1905 or 1906. Also shown is the GER's other London terminus at Fenchurch Street, along with the NLR's Broad Street station and the SE&CR's major stations at Cannon Street and Blackfriars. GE-390

ABOVE: From a high viewpoint we gaze down the cab road to the main line section of Liverpool Street station. Rebuilt in the late 1980s, the station is today largely hidden from view beneath new developments. It is not generally appreciated now how close it was to Broad Street station, on the left here and showing the arches below the platforms, as well as illustrating the difference in levels between the two stations. The arches gave access to the L&NWR goods station beneath Broad Street.

LEFT: A similar view as interpreted by the artist for Raphael Tuck in this 'Oilette' card from Series II of 'London Railway Stations'. Quoting from the description on the back of the card: '*It is one of the largest stations in London. Besides its main line traffic, from here emanate the suburban lines for Ilford, Epping and other Essex residential centres. The suburban traffic is enormous.*' RT702

ABOVE: This superb study of the exterior of Liverpool Street from A. & G.Taylor's 'Reality' Series has so much going on. The dray on the left is not identified but the next vehicle is a very neat van clearly painted up for the Royal Mail. Ahead of that is a London & North Western Railway parcels dray. which in turn is preceded by a horse bus. Behind the mail van is the entrance to Liverpool Street West Side Suburban while the next two gates are Way In and Way Out for the main line. To the left is the sign over the road leading to the L&NWR's Broad Street goods station. In the selection of pedestrians there is only one woman and she is hidden behind the man in uniform in the left foreground. The photographer was positioned at the junction of New Broad Street and Liverpool Street.

RIGHT: Opened in 1884 as the Great Eastern Hotel, the building was extended in 1901 and renamed the Liverpool Street Hotel. The architects for the original building were Charles Barry and his brother Edward Middleton Barry, with Robert W. Edis handling the later extension work. This rather careworn view of the buffet room shows the great detail used in decorating the interior of the hotel, which is still open today, owned by the Hyatt Group and renamed the Andaz London Liverpool Street. The cards in this series were re-printed several times, by Photochrom (as here), Jarrold's of Norwich and the London firm of J.J. Keliher.

THE BUFFET, ABERCORN ROOMS. LIVERPOOL STREET HOTEL

PREVIOUS PAGE BOTTOM: This picture is worth looking at for the departure board alone, with the list of destinations served from the west side departure platforms including a number of places that have long since ceased to be served from Liverpool Street. The times of the next train for each destination were shown by clock face indicators. Behind this was the Gentlemen's Lavatory and Dressing Rooms. The card is by H.M. & S.L. and was posted in May 1908 but the photograph was probably taken a little earlier, circa 1904.

BELOW: The juxtaposition of these two cards here is quite deliberate, with H.M.& S.L. also being responsible for this picture of the east side platforms. Posted in November 1905, this picture is certainly from 1904 as there is a poster advertising the opening of the Kelvedon & Tollesbury Light Railway in October of that year. At the time of these views and following its rebuilding and expansion in the early 1890s, Liverpool Street had eighteen platforms in total, making it the largest station in London until the rebuilding of the South Eastern & Chatham Railway's Victoria station in 1908.

LIVERPOOL STREET STATION H.M.& S.L.

Situated between the two views just seen of the east and west side platforms were the longer main line platforms, which were spanned by a footbridge that took passengers across most of the station. With some of its front end metalwork burnished and shining, 4-4-0 No. 1853 has had the train it arrived with taken away and will no doubt move out to the turntable shortly. A member of GER Class 'D56' (after the order number under which they were constructed), No. 1853 was built in December 1903 as an oil burner but is seen here quite clearly with a tender loaded with coal, the conversion having happened by 1911. Although with many detail differences, the 110 4-4-0s in the number series from 1790-1899 built between 1900 and 1911, were all known as 'Clauds' after the first engine built, No. 1900 *Claud Hamilton*. A futher ten were constructed in 1923, with larger boilers and numbered 1780-89; emerging from works in L&NER green, they were known as 'Super Clauds'. No. 1853 had a long career but changed identity several times, being rebuilt to L&NER Class 'D16/1' as No. 8853, rebuilt to Class '16/2' in 1929, renumbered as No. 2544 in 1929, rebuilt to Class '16/2' in 1946, rebuilt to Class '16/3' in 1947 and then becoming No. 62544 under BR after Nationalisation. It lasted the longest of the 'D56' Series of 'Clauds' in service, being withdrawn in November 1959. The coaching stock on view appears to be mostly 6-wheeled, with a high proportion of Third Class accommodation. The card is from the 'Locomotive Magazine' Series but is not numbered.

RIGHT: Just setting off from Liverpool Street is No. 1008, one of the 'D27' Class of 2-2-2 express engines. Note the tank on the tender, as this was one of the six members of the class fitted for oil burning and with water scoop tenders to enable them to work non-stop to Cromer. Built in 1893, No. 1008 had a life of only ten years, being scrapped in 1903, as the new bogie carriages that were being introduced meant heavier trains, which were too great a load for such small locomotives. On the left is another small engine but one which had a much longer career, courtesy of being enlarged; 'T19' Class 2-4-0 No. 745 was built in 1889 but was rebuilt as a 4-4-0 in 1906, became L&NER Class 'D13' No. 7745 in 1924 and lasted in service until 1933.

LIVERPOOL STREET STATION.

ABOVE AND BELOW: The 'Norfolk Coast Express' leaving Liverpool Street behind GER Class 'S46' or 'Claud Hamilton' 4-4-0 No. 1888. These larger engines quickly replaced the 'D27' Class on top expresses. No. 1888 was built in June 1901 and having been rebuilt three times was finally withdrawn as British Railways No. 62519 in January 1957. This fine F. Moore colour postcard was clearly approved of by the Great Eastern Railway, as they overprinted it several times for their own use. This example was for the District Goods Manager's Office (F. Saward) and was used in December 1912. GE-460

IDEAL HOME EXHIBITION SOUVENIR.

Printing "The Daily Mail."—The Special Trains.

During the last five years The Daily Mail has inaugurated at enormous expense a number of special expresses, starting about two hours earlier than the ordinary news-paper trains, so that there are now few important towns within five hours of London where The Daily Mail cannot be obtained by breakfast time. The latest of these specials was an East Anglian express, costing £6,000 a year, by means of which Norwich received its papers over two hours earlier. Ipswich two and a half, Yarmouth three hours and a quarter, and many smaller towns four hours earlier. Similar special trains are run over the other principal railway lines.

POST CARD

FOR COMMUNICATION.

Telephone No.;
LONDON WALL 3341
Telegraphic Address:
"RAILROADING, LONDON."

FOR ADDRESS ONLY.

GREAT EASTERN RAILWAY.

When replying
please quote
this reference.
DISTRICT GOODS MANAGER'S OFFICE,
23, HAMILTON HOUSE,
183, BISHOPSGATE, LONDON, E.C.

No. 1018/44422

29/2/ 1912

Subject Elg Case Ex Royd

I beg to acknowledge the receipt of your
letter of the C22/2., which
shall have my attention.

Yours obediently,
F. SAWARD,
District Goods Manager.

Published by The Locomotive Publishing Co., Ltd., 3 Amen Corner, London, E.C.

Mess Speirs Pond
35 new Bruge st
EC

The Norfolk Coast Express leaving Liverpool Street, G. E. Railway

ABOVE: Publicity for the *Daily Mail* and for the Great Eastern Railway. An unidentified 'Claud Hamilton' 4-4-0 starts from Liverpool Street on the 'Daily Mail Special Train' just introduced on the Great Eastern line. As the text below the picture indicates, such new services – of which there were several – were effectively sponsored by the *Daily Mail* to ensure that different parts of the country received their newspapers in time for them to reach their breakfast readers. The card was produced for the 1908 Ideal Home Exhibition and posted that November.

ABOVE AND RIGHT: Although not yet polluted by the fumes of motor traffic, London was a dirty city and had suffered problems from air pollution for centuries, much of it caused in earlier times by poor sanitation. This resulted in the 'Great Stink' of the mid 19th century and the subsequent building of the capital's sewage system. The main culprit by the dawn of the 20th century were now the huge number of coal fires – every home had one – along with the railways and their engine sheds, and not forgetting all of the industries which relied on steam power, including for the production of gas and electricity.

This smoke laden atmosphere could combine lethally with cold damp weather to cause a 'smog'. This culminated in the five day 'Great Smog' of December 1952, which modern research now estimates caused up to 12,000 deaths and which led directly to a concerted effort to clean up London's air. Printed for use by the Office of the Superintendent of the Line, this poster, 'A Step in the Bright Direction', makes a great contrast between London, with the murky picture of St. Paul's, and the sunny delights of the East Coast. The card dates from circa 1912. GE-402

RIGHT AND BELOW: The original London terminus for what was then the Eastern Counties Railway was opened as Shoreditch on 1st July 1840. The name was changed to Bishopsgate on 27th July 1846 and it served as the terminus until the Great Eastern Railway, as the company had now become, opened Liverpool Street station on 2nd February 1874. Bishopsgate was now closed as a passenger station, although it is understood that a few trains continued to use it over the next five years. Bishopsgate was rebuilt as the fine looking goods station illustrated here on a Great Eastern Railway poster reproduction. Overprinted with a correspondence back, the postcard was used by the Goods Manager's Office at Liverpool Street station shortly before the First World War, posted on 2nd May 1913. Closure of the goods station came about in December 1964, following a serious fire. GE-403.

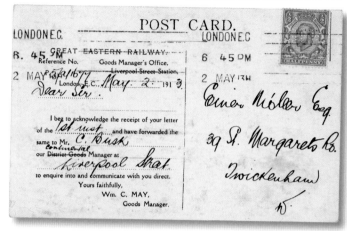

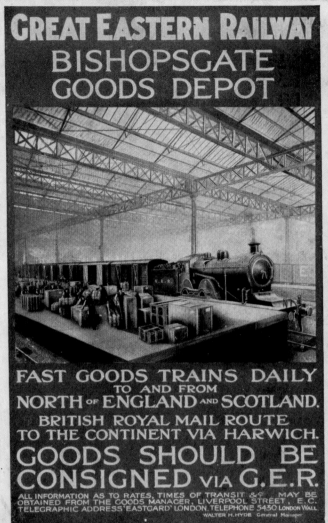

BELOW: A scene like this would have been quite common in Edwardian times. These Coffee & Cocoa stands were supported by the Temperance movement and were intended to provide non-alcoholic refreshment to workers. The card was posted at Paddock Wood in September 1908 and is noted as being outside Bishopsgate station. Unfortunately, there is nothing in the picture to confirm this with just the word 'RAILWAY' visible top left, along with three men in what could well be railway uniforms. Nor does the publisher, W. Hagelberg, help as he operated in London, New York and Berlin. We would love to hear if anyone can confirm the location.

COFFEE & COCOA STALL. 3490

Published in 1905 in the 'Locomotive Magazine Series', this view of the top of Bethnal Green bank was taken from Bethnal Green West Junction signal box. The bank was the hill to be climbed to get out of the terminus and a local train heading for North Woolwich is just reaching the end of the ascent, whilst a similar service is just commencing the journey down. On the left is Spitalfields goods depot (originally called Brick Lane depot) and in the left background is one of the two large granaries built here by 1850 (the other is off picture to the left). In the smokey haze between the goods wagons and the granary building can just be made out the superstructure over the wagon hoist, which lowered wagons to the street level goods depot below. The three lines that pass just to the right of the granary cross the main line behind the steam from the Woolwich train as they head to Bishopsgate goods depot. Between the wagons on the left and Whitechapel signal box, a line curved off to the left at ninety degrees to serve Spitalfields coal depot. Beyond the left-hand end of the gantry, Spitalfields Granary signal box is just discernible.

We now turn the other way to see Bethnal Green West Junction signal box (from which the previous photograph was taken), on card No. 1717 in the same series and probably taken on the same day, albeit this print from the negative was produced at a slightly later date and with far less use of the sepia toning chemicals. Two local trains are heading for Liverpool Street with Bethnal Green Junction station framed by three sets of tall bracket signals. The train on the right has yet to be signalled and tracing carefully along the track you can see that the points are set for a different route. Normally part of a signalman's duty was to record the time for each train but with as many as 128 trains in an hour passing Bethnal Green Junction, he was relieved of this task and a second cabin was provided just for the timekeeper; this can be seen behind the signals on the right. It is believed that this cabin was erected in 1891 and, remarkably, part of the communication here was the guard shouting the train number to the timekeeper! 'Junction' was apparently dropped from the station's name in 1946, since when it has been plain Bethnal Green.

RIGHT: As with so many of Mr Pouteau's cards, this one is somewhat faded (it is likely that he was rather parsimonious with the fixative!) but modern computer technology now allows us to retrieve much of what was in the image, which gives a good view of the Ipswich platforms at Bethnal Green (on the right of the previous view). The station was opened on 24th May 1874 as Bethnal Green Junction, the change to plain Bethnal Green coming about in December 1946, when the only platforms in use were those serving the Cambridge line, so the dropping of 'Junction' was a sensible move. The height of the signals ensured that they did not get hidden from view by the station buildings.

Coborn Road, Station Bow.

LEFT: Coborn Road was 1^1/$_4$ miles beyond Bethnal Green, on the way to Stratford. Opened in December 1883, the station closed during the First World War, on 22nd May 1916, reopening on 5th May 1919. Final closure took place on 8th December 1946, after which Stratford became the first calling point for trains on this route. The view is the first of a number showing the stations on this route by Charles Martin and here he has captured for us one of the long, saw-toothed, arched awnings typical of many of the Great Eastern suburban stations. This generous provision is not reflected by the lack of passengers but this was probably a Sunday, whilst the train running in is heading for Liverpool Street. This was a resited station, as it was originally on the east side of Coborn Road, moved probably at the time extra tracks were laid in on the main line, in spite of which it still had just the two platforms shown here. The full name of the station was Coborn Road for Old Ford.

Cambridge Heath Station. N. E.

LEFT: Cambridge Heath is the first stop north of Bethnal Green on the Cambridge line and the station is seen here from Cambridge Road, with Hackney Road leading away under the bridge. Opened on 27th May 1872, the station closed for the same period in the Great War as Coborn Road and was also closed for a month early in 1986. This latter closure may have been when the buildings seen here were replaced by an unattractive modern entrance. The station is open today but facilities are limited.

LONDON FIELDS STATION.

LEFT: Opening the same day as Cambridge Heath, the next station north is London Fields, the name taken from the nearby public park which is still there today. London Fields also closed from 22nd May 1916 to 1st July 1919 and then again on 13th November 1981 but was reopened on 29th September 1986. A shorter version of the standard canopy was provided on the two platforms and there were two more lines on the east side that were not served. A local bound for Liverpool Street is calling circa 1904 and it seems to have been normal practice for engines to run bunker first in this direction. Writing in 1907, C.J. Allen noted that the station names in this area ending in Green, Fields, Heath and Downs suggested an elysium hardly in keeping with the dingy streets of factories and tenements that surround them. In mitigation he noted that London Fields and Hackney Downs still remained, as they do 110 years later.

HACKNEY DOWNS JUNCTION

ABOVE: Hackney Downs Junction officially dropped 'Junction' from its name in 1896, although it seems from this picture it did not vanish overnight. The station had four platforms, these two serving the Enfield line, and was a busy location, with nearly 100 trains in each direction every day. This was of course less than today, with the line now electrified and with modern signalling; in 1907 trains were all steam hauled and signals mechanically controlled from the numerous signal boxes. The picture is by F.E. Mackay, published by Pouteau and, along with the view right, featured in the 1907 article by C.J. Allen published in *The Railway Magazine*.

RIGHT: From another faded card, we have crossed to the Cambridge line platforms where the station master posed for Mr Mackay. The station had opened on 27th May 1872 and this view is to the south. Today, changes have been made, in part to accommodate electrification but it has managed to retain the look of a proper station with no bus shelters to be seen.

RIGHT: Hackney Downs exterior looking east along Dalston Lane on a clearly sunny day, with a well dressed lady on the right carefully protecting herself from the sun. The station entrance was fairly well hidden but the prominent sign and pointing finger on the bridge gave an indication as to where it could be found. The remarkably ornate street lamp is worthy of note and the road transport is once again all horse powered. Note too the street vendors, with a newspaper stand on the left beneath the protection of the bridge span and what looks to be a fruit & veg stall in the right foreground. This Charles Martin card dates from circa 1905.

Hackney Down Station   Dalston Lane   N. E.

HACKNEY DOWNS JUNCTION.

LEFT: An animated view on the platform at Hackney Downs, with two gentlemen in top hats accompanied by a pair of well dressed ladies awaiting the train for Liverpool Street. The route discs on the engines utilised two colours, green or white, with the position indicating which route the train was on. Again the engine heading in the Up direction is running bunker first. The close-coupled 4-wheeled carriages at the Down platform do not look too comfortable, being narrower than modern stock and with the seating squeezed in at five to a side.

RIGHT: Running in from the south, this circa 1905 Charles Martin card belies the rule, as the engine is running bunker first in the Down direction but it is not possible to read what is on the headboard. Clapton station opened on 1st July 1872 and the buildings on the bridge face on to Upper Clapton Road. The booking office on the left remains, although it has lost the chimneys and some of the platform buildings also still survive.

Clapton Station.   N. E.

RIGHT: The decorated engine and watching crowd tell us that Royalty were passing by here but who? It could well be the Duke of York's Wedding Special, which dates the picture to 6th July 1893. The stock and engine look to be extremely well cleaned, the latter being a 'T19' Class 2-4-0 fitted for oil burning, probably No. 761 which was a regular royal train engine and certainly hauled the Duke's special. The location is probably between Clapton Junction and Copper Mills Junction, with the train crossing Walthamstow Marshes. No. 761 was built in 1890 and withdrawn in September 1908, whilst the card was published by the LPC circa 1910.

BELOW: The next station after Rectory Road is Stoke Newington, with a Liverpool Street train running in captured by Charles Martin around 1905. The entrance and booking office are now housed in an uninspiring modern flat roof structure, typical of the early 1980s, whilst at platform level the canopies have been removed and the shelters match the booking office. Very often the advertisements were not just the usual big companies and would include those of local concerns, such as the Hackney General Drapers on the left.

Stoke Newington. - Rectory Road Station.

LEFT: This Rectory Road view can be dated to early 1905, from the newspaper billboards referring to the fall of Port Arthur in the Russo-Japanese War. Usually when it is possible to read the information displayed in this way it is something of no help in dating the view but this is a useful exception.

Stoke Newington Station. G. E. R.

RIGHT: The Great Eastern building seen here at the entrance to Stoke Newington survived until about 1980, when the present structure was built. No horse cabs (note the licence plates) will be waiting these days but the building on the right remains. As with the interior view, this card, posted in 1908, is again by Charles Martin.

Stoke Newington Station. N. (G. E. R y.)

BOTTOM: The GER opened the station at Seven Sisters on 22nd July 1872, as an intermediate stop on the Enfield Town Branch, on the right where the usual saw-tooth canopy can be seen in the distance. The canopies on the Palace Gates Branch platforms, opened in 1878, were of a much simpler style. The original station entrance was situated at the north end of the Enfield platforms but was closed when the Victoria Line opened. A foot crossing can be seen leading from the end of the Up Enfield platform and old maps show what appears to be a subway just beyond this, where a small building can be seen on the Down platform. Unfortunately it is not possible to make out the wording on the notice. The same map shows the odd looking building behind the men as a signal box, although it does not look the slightest bit like one. The presence of a soldier with the staff suggests this may be a 1914-18 view.

RIGHT: Further to the east is the Lea Valley line where, on 15th September 1840, the Northern & Eastern Railway opened a station on the north side of the Lea Bridge Road bridge. The station was reasonably enough opened as Lea Bridge Road but 'Road' was dropped from the name in April 1871. In the end the only trains serving the station were the Tottenham Hale to North Woolwich service, which was withdrawn in July 1985 and Lea Bridge, latterly an unstaffed halt, was closed. Just over twenty years later the station has been rebuilt and is back in use. The Northern and Eastern Railway had been built to the gauge of 5ft but this was soon changed to the standard 4ft $8^1/_2$ in gauge, the work being completed in 1844. It is also worth noting that the station is believed to have been the first to have been built with the main building situated on the bridge, later quite a common feature. This is the limit of our exploration of the lines from Liverpool Street.

LEA BRIDGE STATION, Great Eastern Railway.

SEVEN. SISTERS. JUNCTION.

S 5080 FENCHURCH STREET GREAT EASTERN RAILWAY STATION FACING EAST

6
FENCHURCH STREET

GER, LT&SR and Millwall Dock Railway

ABOVE: A view of the Fenchurch Street concourse in about 1910, although there are no useful boards on the bookstall to help with the date. The card is in the W.H. Smith Kingsway Series and would have been sold from this bookstall. To the left, in front of the telegraph office, the Great Eastern Railway departures make interesting reading. All are services long gone, some as early as 1926. The sheeting in the roof girders above suggests painting or other work was is in progress and there are two slot machines to be seen, one giving no clue as to what it might be vending but the other dispensing Nestlé's chocolate.

RIGHT: This coloured card in the 'Locomotive Publishing Series' shows us the different liveries of the GER on the left and the London, Tilbury & Southend Railway on the right. Today, the roof has been totally replaced thanks to the office building constructed above the station but the 1841 station frontage has been retained. Note the ducts designed to take smoke away, in an attempt to keep the station clear. However, two of the three engines are nowhere near them and columns of smoke can be seen!

RIGHT: This might be described as the other entrance to Fenchurch Street. It was situated at the corner of John Street and Coopers Row, through a building now demolished in the redevelopment of the area. At some point in time by the early 1950s, John Street became Crosswall. There is still an entrance here but it is now situated under the bridge at the right edge of this picture. The station was opened on 2nd August 1841 by the London & Blackwall Railway, which became part of the Great Eastern Railway in 1866. The sign above the door puts the Great Eastern at the top, with the later arrival, the LT&SR, at the bottom. By contrast today, there are no longer services from Fenchurch Street to any of the ex-GER destinations. The main entrance, Grade II listed, was situated in Railway Place, a name now changed to Fenchurch Place.

Trains for Ongar and Southend await departure from Fenchurch Street, showing the overall roof in the background, in a view taken circa 1910 that does the station no favours at all in terms of its appearance; it looks decidedly dirty, dingy and down at heel. A fifth platform had been added in 1883, tucked away on the right here at the outer end of the station and used by North Greenwich and Blackwall trains. The station was remodelled in 1935, when the number of platforms was again reduced to four, as a result of the platform on the left here being extended in both length and width, and the centre road being removed. The LT&SR named almost all their engines, this one being '51' Class 4-4-2T No. 57 *Crouch Hill*, built by Sharp, Stewart & Co. in 1900. Sadly, the Midland Railway did not continue this practice when they took the LT&SR over in 1912 and names quickly vanished. No. 57 became nameless MR No. 2164 and then No. 2098 under the LM&SR; it was allotted No. 41916 by British Railways but was withdrawn in March 1951 before the number was applied. The Great Eastern engine is Holden 'M15' Class 2-4-2T No. 80, the last of the class completed in May 1909 and withdrawn in February 1936 as L&NER No. 7080.

Right at the end of our period is this view of Leman Street, taken in 1924. The station opened on 1st June 1877, was closed from May 1916 to July 1919 as a war-time economy measure and closed again on 7th July 1942, this time not to reopen. It was rebuilt in the mid-1890s as part of the widening between Fenchurch Street and Stepney and the last vestiges vanished with the Docklands Light Railway construction in 1985. The train is from Blackwall, hauled by GER 0-6-0T No. 155, built at Stratford in 1889. Classified by the L&NER as 'J65' and surviving into BR days, withdrawal was not until November 1953. It is difficult to see here but the engine is running as a 2-4-0T with the front section of the coupling rod removed, one of a number of the class so treated. The card is from Horne's Camera Mart in Old Broad Street but may well be a private print just for the photographer, L.A. Blount.

Moving east to dockland, an area now a major financial district, we find Millwall Dock Railway engines, in a scene at South Dock station where, as usual, the staff, all employed by the dock company, are posing for the photographer. The engine, No. 3, was built by Manning, Wardle in 1880, Works No. 749 and was delivered with No. 4, MW Works No. 750, built at the same time. Such very small locomotives were required because weights on the line were strictly limited by the presence of three wooden swing bridges. The station was opened as part of the Millwall Extension Railway's line on 18th December 1871 but from July 1881 to May 1895 it was known as South West India Dock. It was closed on 4th May 1926, the line's passenger service falling victim partly to the competition from electric trams and buses, but also in part because people were moving out from the area to live in some of the developing suburbs. In a further blow to the line's fortunes, the buildings seen here had been destroyed by fire in 1917. The MER was opened as part of the London & Blackwall Railway, which had been leased to the GER in 1865 but the line was run between Millwall Junction and North Greenwich by the dock company, in connection with the GER service from Fenchurch Street to Blackwall. The card was issued by the Locomotive Publishing Company in 1905.

RIGHT: Captioned 'Cubitt Town Station', this was the terminus of the Millwall Extension Railway and was officially called North Greenwich, which the company thought was more up-market than Cubitt Town. The engine is another by Manning, Wardle and could be No. 6. Note that Greenwich was one of the destinations on the departure board at Fenchurch Street. These last two stations were both in the dock area that occupied much of the Isle of Dogs, an area which has changed completely in recent years. Both coal and water were available at the station which, although mainly of wooden construction survived for many years after closure as a store and then used by a boat club; it was finally demolished in 1969. Perkins & Sons of Lewisham had ventured across the river for this view, which has had its background cropped or painted out.

ABOVE: Perkins had a useful trip from Lewisham, and here is another view he took at North Greenwich, again captioned as Cubitt Town. Clearly a sister engine, it is soon possible to spot detail differences – the brake pipe on the opposite side of the front coupling for instance – but it has not been possible to identify which of the Manning, Wardle 2-4-0T passenger engines this is.

LEFT: Another shot of a Manning, Wardle tank at the very end of the line at North Greenwich, on a card published by Pouteau circa 1906. The Millwall engines were serviced here but there were no goods facilities. There was a ferry across the river to Greenwich but this ceased to operate when the foot tunnel was opened by the London County Council on 4th August 1902. The distant towers to the left are the Royal Naval College. Situated at the southern point of the Isle of Dogs but on the north bank of the Thames, this North Greenwich should not be confused with the present day North Greenwich Pier, which is on the opposite side of the river (see page 191).

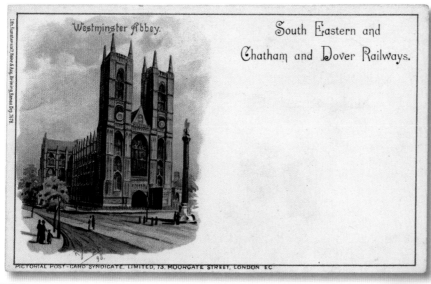

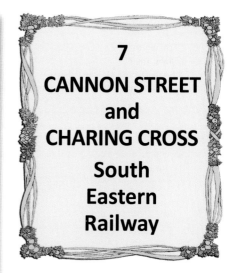

7
CANNON STREET and CHARING CROSS
South Eastern Railway

ABOVE LEFT: Moving to the south-east of London, the first lines to be explored are those served by the South Eastern Railway. We begin with a picture of Westminster Abbey, another example from a series of cards sold in slot machines at stations (see front title page). The cards were printed with the name of the appropriate company and thus provided advertising as part of the agreement for allowing the slot machines to be installed. They cost one halfpenny (a 'ha'penny' as they used to be called) or one penny if already stamped. The cards in this set are again signed R. Joust and dated 1898 but no further details about the artist have come to light. The odd combined title for the 'South Eastern and Chatham and Dover Railways' tells us that the amalgamation that produced the South Eastern & Chatham Railway was afoot. SE-805.

ABOVE: Regent Street about 1905 looking no less crowded than today but with just a single motor car almost hidden amongst all of the horse-drawn vehicles. On the left, an SE&CR covered dray is about to pass the establishment of Dickens & Jones, a familiar sight in Regent Street until 2007, although they had moved from the premises seen here in 1922.

ABOVE AND LEFT: Produced by the SE&CR around 1912, this sketch map showed their main goods depots in London. Not exactly to scale, these cards were used by the Goods Department, in this instance from Bricklayers Arms, to acknowledge correspondence. Clearly it was aimed at businesses and not produced for collectors to display in their albums. The printer was McCorquodale & Co. Ltd, who undertook printing for a number of railways. SE-059.

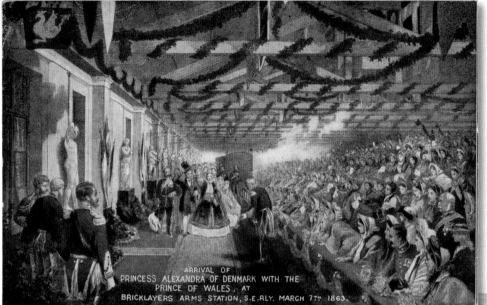

ARRIVAL OF PRINCESS ALEXANDRA OF DENMARK WITH THE PRINCE OF WALES, AT BRICKLAYERS ARMS STATION, S.E.RLY. MARCH 7TH 1863.

LEFT AND BELOW LEFT: Bricklayers Arms was originally the passenger terminus, operating in that capacity from 1st May 1844 to 31st January 1852, when the line through towards Charing Cross was opened. After 1852, when it became a goods station as seen on the map card, occasional use was made on special occasions and for excursion traffic. Here the station is decked out for the arrival of Princess Alexandra of Denmark and the Prince of Wales on 7th March 1863. The card was used by the Goods Department and specifically printed for Bricklayers Arms Station, about 1910. SE-058

BELOW: Another card for the SE&CR Goods Department provides us a final look at Bricklayers Arms goods station, showing the entrance situated on the Old Kent Road. The design of the station was by Lewis Cubitt and the central tower on the main façade may be glimpsed through the gate. SE-057

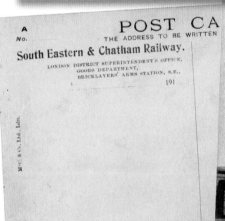

A
No.
POST CA
THE ADDRESS TO BE WRITTEN
South Eastern & Chatham Railway.
LONDON DISTRICT SUPERINTENDENT'S OFFICE,
GOODS DEPARTMENT,
BRICKLAYERS' ARMS STATION, S.E.,
191

BRICKLAYERS ARMS GENERAL GOODS STATION. OLD KENT ROAD. S.E.

CHARING CROSS STATION. FOLKESTONE EXPRESS.

RIGHT: Charing Cross was the goal of the South Eastern Railway, for establishing a terminus north of the River Thames. From the Raphael Tuck Series No. 9279, 'London Railway Stations', this delightful view depicts a scene beneath the original roof of the station, designed by Sir John Hawkshaw. The picture would date from 1903 or 1904, a year or so before the unfortunate problem with the roof. The train is one of the Continental boat expresses and provides a delightful study of the dress of the period. A careful look at the posters above the train shows that Tucks have included an advertisement for their postcards.

RIGHT: Charing Cross station was opened on 11th January 1864, with E.M. Barry's hotel opening in May the following year. King Edward I had twelve crosses erected in 1291-94, in memory of his wife Eleanor of Castile, marking the nightly stops along the route taken when transporting her body to London. The Eleanor Cross here was a replica erected in 1865 by the SER and not in the same place as the original, in Whitehall just off Trafalgar Square, destroyed in 1647 during the Civil War. The hotel is still recognisable and up to the fourth floor is pretty much unchanged. Above that, the top two floors are now much plainer and the decorative roof line is no more. Unlike the establishments at Holborn Viaduct and Cannon Street, the hotel was repaired following war damage suffered in 1941. Sold in 1983, it is now run by Amba Hotels and the building is Grade II listed.

LEFT: A fine view of the outer end of the station, showing the old roof, in a view first published on a printed card in 1904 but this photographic version provides much clearer detail. Ready for departure is 'D' Class 4-4-0 No. 92, signalled clear to head out over Hungerford Bridge. Built by Dübs & Co. in March 1903, the locomotive's first allocation was to Bricklayers Arms shed. Many of the 'D' Class were rebuilt to 'D1' in the 1920s but No. 92 was not amongst those so treated and, indeed, seems to have led a fairly uneventful life, being withdrawn as BR No. 31092 in June 1951. On the right, we can identify the 'F' Class 4-4-0 as No. 233 courtesy of the oval numberplate mounted on the rear of its tender. The final member of the class to be built, at Ashford Works in March 1898, it was rebuilt to 'F1' in June 1913 and withdrawn in March 1937.

Charing Cross Station (Interior). London.

LEFT: This anonymous printed postcard provides us with a great view of the interior of the station, with every platform apparently occupied. In the centre, a Class 'F' 4-4-0 has arrived while a number of horse-drawn cabs wait for custom on the cab road. An impressive lamp is suspended from the roof and one more of the same type can just be seen in the centre right background. Further lighting came from a series of lamp standards on the platforms. Two parcels carriages stand at the end of the nearer platform, with doors wide open, waiting to be loaded.

On 5th of December 1905, one of the tie rods in the roof at Charing Cross fractured as a result of a manufacturing flaw. Fortunately, the accident happened mid-afternoon before the evening rush, so that in spite of a 70 foot length of it collapsing on to the platforms below, the only injuries were to three workmen who were on the roof at the time. It was decided to replace rather than repair it, which resulted in the station being closed and it was not reopened until 19th March 1906. Here we see the remains being removed – according to the message on the reverse of the card, this was the last of the old roof to come down. Clearly a head for heights was needed here and scaling those ladders would have been something! The view is looking south, with the bulk of the Hotel Metropole in the left and centre background, and part of the Hotel Victoria in the right background, both of which fronted on to Northumberland Avenue; they now operate as the Corinthia Hotel and the Club Quarters Hotel respectively.

One of the fine coloured cards by the Locomotive Publishing Company shows us the outer end of the new roof, emblazoned with the initials and the company crest of the SE&CR. Providing a contrast in 4-4-0s, on the left is 'F' Class No. 60, new in October 1891, whilst on the right is No. 591, the last 'D' class, built in March 1907. No. 60 was rebuilt to 'F1' in November 1905 and survived until April 1946, whilst No. 591 was another of the 'D' Class not rebuilt and withdrawn as BR No. 31591 in May 1955.

Used by Oliver Arc Lamp Limited to advertise their 'Oriflamme' lamps – the lettering was painted directly on to the glass plate negative – this card shows well how the new roof changed the appearance of the station. The card was sent to the Corporation Electricity Works, Bridlington, Yorkshire. This was a popular method of advertising, showing the product in use rather than set up in a showroom. Charles Oliver established the company in 1898 in Finsbury, specialising in the supply of lamps to railway companies and relocated the growing business to larger premises in Woolwich in 1900. The business had become Oliver Pell Control Ltd by 1960 and is now owned by C&S Controls Ltd of Bexleyheath. The 0-4-4T is not identifiable but has a star burnished on its smokebox door, a practice that was particularly popular with Scottish enginemen. The date on the postmark is unreadable but the picture would have been taken circa 1906-07.

"ORIFLAMME" LAMPS
Charing Cross S.E & C.R.

RIGHT: Much has changed at Cannon Street since this card was published in 1904, No. 1 in the 'Locomotive Magazine Series', but at least the twin towers remain. The roof seen here has long since been replaced and there is now a garden above the platforms. Several engines may be seen, with their green livery contrasting with the duller colours of the station. The signal box straddling all of the approach lines was removed when new electric signalling was installed in 1926, tied in with the introduction of electric trains. Cannon Street station opened on 1st September 1866, the SER having first had to construct the bridge seen here, to carry the extension of their line from London Bridge across the River Thames to the north bank.

Cannon Street Station S.E.&C.R.

ABOVE: Probably published around 1910, this LPC card reveals the wooden construction of the platforms and also shows the decorative lamp and station sign, leaving no doubt as to where we are. Both the engines seen date from 1900. To the left, London, Chatham & Dover Railway Class 'M3' 4-4-0 was allocated their No. 26 but went straight into the SE&CR series as No. 485. Reboilered in 1909, withdrawal came in July 1927. Rather longer lived was 'C' Class 0-6-0 No. 715, which was built in December 1900 and, as BR No. 31715, lasted in service until November 1961. When new, No. 715 was allocated to Bricklayers Arms shed.

LEFT: A similar LPC view but in colour, showing more of the overall roof and towers, and again featuring No. 485.

RIGHT: Published in the Wrench Series, this view of Cannon Street Hotel and the station also shows the District Railway station almost crouching in the foreground. The SER station had the ground floor whilst the hotel, originally the City Terminus Hotel, occupied the rest of the building; renaming took place in 1879. The hotel suffered war damage in 1941 and was closed. It had been used as offices for the previous ten years, and was eventually demolished in 1960, a modern office block now occupying the site.

BELOW: Spa Road & Bermondsey was opened in 1867 by the SER and was renamed Spa Road, Bermondsey ten years later. The station was closed on 15th March 1915 but was used by staff until 21st September 1925. This was the second station, the original being a couple of hundred yards to the west. The relocation was as a result of the widening of the line which took place before the First World War. The arches are still to be seen today.

BELOW: Originally a terminus, Maze Hill for Greenwich was opened by the SER as Greenwich (Maze Hill) on 1st January 1873. On the North Kent line heading towards London, the SER was awaiting the completion of Greenwich Tunnel, allowing the line to be connected with the London & Greenwich Railway, which had served the area since 1838. The name was changed to Maze Hill & East Greenwich on 1st February 1878, and then to Maze Hill & Greenwich Park on 1st July. From 1st January 1879 it became Maze Hill (East Greenwich) or Maze Hill & East Greenwich, with 'For National Maritime Museum' added in July 1937. This view on the Down platform, looking south-east, thus shows a name that does not tie in with any of the above. Today it is plain Maze Hill, the station having been rebuilt in the early 1970s following a fire. This anonymous view dates from around 1905.

LEFT: On the more southerly route to Dartford was the station at Lewisham Junction, which was opened by the SER on 1st January 1857. It replaced the original 1849 station, allowing the Mid-Kent line to be served west of the Lewisham Road bridge and 'Junction' was dropped from the name from 7th July 1929. There are now two additional platforms served by the Docklands Light Railway. Produced by Perkins & Son of Lewisham, the card was posted in August 1911 and the photographer has certainly made a good job of capturing a busy scene, with many clearly aware and standing still for the picture. The station has survived remarkably intact but is not protected by any heritage listing.

RIGHT: Published circa 1908 by Perkins of Lewisham, this view of Catford Bridge station was taken many years earlier. It probably dates from the 1880s, as there is no signal box visible at the far end of the Up platform; it is understood that this box was installed around 1890. The gentleman in top hat and frock coat could well be the station master. Planting along the wall on the left precludes the usual array of advertising and there is a neat garden on the right. Looking north from the Catford Road bridge, the houses in Doggett Road can be seen on the east side of the line. The bridge from which this rural view was taken has been rebuilt and now carries a section of the South Circular road and, unsurprisingly, the area has been much developed from the scene here.

A bit of Old Catford.—Catford Station, S.E.

RIGHT: The SER opened Catford Bridge, on the Mid Kent line, on 1st January 1857. The station is situated on Adenmore Road but although the building remains it is no longer in railway use. It is still quite recognisable but the neat little shop has gone and the coal office is boarded up. The platforms, as at so many stations, have been considerably lengthened to cater for the longer trains needed today, whilst the coal yard, served by a single siding and just glimpsed here through the gateway, is now buried beneath several large blocks of flats. We shall return to Catford Bridge in a few pages time, via the London, Chatham & Dover Railway's line.

Catford Bridge Station.

LONDON CHATHAM & DOVER RAILWAY COMPANY.

CHEAPSIDE. LOOKING WEST.

THE PICTURE POST CAR

LEFT: One of a series of probably ten cards that date from 1898, produced by The Picture Postcard Company Ltd and which were for sale in slot machines. This one is looking to the west along Cheapside, with the Mansion House just behind the photographer. LCD-827.

BELOW: Holborn Viaduct was opened by the LC&DR on 1st August 1874, providing the company with a station convenient for the City. The hotel followed three years later in November 1877 but, after forty years of service, it was closed and the building was used as offices from 1917, although the ground floor refreshment rooms remained in use until 1931. The end came in 1941, the hotel being a war-time casualty and demolished as a result of the damage sustained. The card was published by Stengel & Co. and posted in November 1909.

8
HOLBORN VIADUCT
and
BLACKFRIARS
London, Chatham & Dover Railway

BELOW: Looking into Holborn Viaduct platforms in October 1913. At this date the station was known as Holborn Viaduct High Level, a change which took place on 1st May 1912, but the name reverted to plain Holborn Viaduct from 1st June 1916. Closure took place on 29th January 1990, it having been made pretty much redundant by the Thameslink service and the nearby station on that line.

Holborn Viaduct Hotel, London.

Another victim of Thameslink was the bridge at the bottom of Ludgate Hill, where the line now runs below ground. Neatly posed for the photographer is one of the SE&CR 'Q1' Class 0-4-4T locomotives, fitted with condenser gear for running through the tunnels to King's Cross. The image did not quite manage to 'freeze' the locomotive, so the numberplate is just too blurred to decipher. The card was published by Photochrom and this copy was posted in December 1911 from Southampton to the Isle of Wight. The view was taken from a multi-storey building on the west side of Ludgate Circus, with St. Paul's cathedral towering over the scene in the background, which is still quite recognisable today. City Thameslink station now occupies the area to the right of and beneath the bridge in the foreground but otherwise, the property on the right still survives largely intact. However, on the opposite side of the street, everything is now modern office blocks and shops up as far as the Guild Church of St. Martin Within, which still remains with its distinctive spire, as do the buildings beyond it.

166 LONDON E. C. — *Ludgate Hill Station and New Bridge Street.* — LL.

2681 ST. PAULS STATION.   LONDON.

ABOVE: Situated on New Bridge Street just to the south of Ludgate Circus, the LC&DR station known as Ludgate Hill was another victim of Thameslink work. This was not the reason for its closure, which had taken place on 3rd March 1929, but did result in its final demolition circa 1990. Note the sign on the building for 'The Picture Postcard', a monthly magazine of the time. This is another busy scene, with a policeman holding up the traffic to allow pedestrians to cross. Also of interest are the two heavily laden carts carrying hay – fodder – which provided the fuel for all the horse-power on show. Huge quantities were required in the capital on a daily basis, providing further traffic for the railways and balancing the by-product being transported back out. LL card No. 166 dates from around 1908 or perhaps a little earlier, as there are no motor vehicles to be seen.

ABOVE: There is still a bridge at the lower end of Queen Victoria Street, although it might well be thought that the present structure is less attractive than the original one seen here. Opened on 10th May 1886, the station was known as St. Paul's until renamed Blackfriars on 1st February 1937. Post Office station on the Central Line was modernised in the 1930s and was renamed St. Paul's at this time. The bridge carries the Thameslink service these days and the station building on the left has been replaced by an office block. The entrance to the station is now round the corner to the left, beyond the bridge.

RIGHT: Blackfriars Bridge has changed considerably from this circa 1908 Raphael Tuck published view. The station, the old roof of which is visible to the left, has been completely rebuilt and now stretches across the river, with an entrance on the south side a recent addition.

BLACKFRIARS BRIDGE & St PAULS, LONDON.

LEFT: Looking from road level to the Up platform at Brixton, it is clear that space was limited here but the station provided a useful covered area in front of the shops built under the railway. The LC&DR opened the station on 25th August 1862 and from 1st May the following year until 9th July it was known as Brixton & South Stockwell. The girder bridge carried the LB&SCR line built in 1867. The covered area was extended past the shops on the left and just before the bridge are the steps giving access to the station. This is a scene still recognisable today.

BELOW: A bold sign indicates the presence of Wandsworth Road station, opened on 1st March 1863, although there is no arrow or pointing finger to show that it was on the right. The walls under the span were plastered with posters which certainly brightened it up a bit and the houses beyond the bridge on the right are still there. Published by Charles Martin, the picture dates from the horse tram era, as evidenced by the deposits of manure in the road!

ATLANTIC ROAD, BRIXTON.

SOUTH EASTERN & CHATHAM RAILWAY.
WANDSWORTH ROAD STATION.

Wandsworth Road S. W.

The Railway Bridges, Brixton Road.

Charles Martin's documenting of London's streets on picture postcards was extensive and, as this second view shows, fortunately extended to many of the suburbs south of the river. Like these two pictures, they are also often packed with interest, showing much historical and social detail. Two bridges are shown here spanning Brixton Road, with the lines of two railway companies being carried across. Shown in the colour view on the previous page, Brixton station is situated just off picture to the right of the second bridge. The nearer bridge with its decorative wrought iron span was on the LB&SCR South London line and both bridges are still used today. Despite there being four electric tramcars in view, a horse-drawn bus is still plying its trade, with three passengers enjoying the delights of the top deck. No destination board is visible, so it can only be surmised that perhaps it served an area that the trams did not. Looking at the tram track, the centre groove for the electric conduit can clearly be seen, the cars picking up the current via a plough-like device. Both bridges look remarkably similar today, with the nearer one still supported on the iron pillars seen here. The card was posted in August 1907.

P.&S. 2760. BROCKLEY STATION.

A confusing title here, for the station is actually Brockley Lane, the LC&DR station and thus not to be mistaken for the LB&SCR's Brockley station, situated close by and which, unlike Brockley Lane, is still open. The station seen here opened in June 1872 and was on the branch between Nunhead and Greenwich Park; it was closed on 1st January 1917 when services on the branch ceased. No details have been found for the publisher, P.&S., and the postmark is illegible but the card was sent with the George V stamp introduced in 1912. To further narrow the date down, the locomotive running in is a member of the LC&DR 'M2' Class, No. 184, which was built in February 1884, rebuilt in January 1903 and withdrawn in December 1912. Note the use of a single signal post carrying arms for both directions. Although the branch had been completely closed, a new connection was put in at Lewisham in 1929 and the line reopened but not the station. In the background is the tower of St. Peters church, which is now without the four pinnacles seen here.

Published y P.S & V., Lewisham

700

View from Lewisham Road Station

Lewisham Road station was situated just on the Greenwich side of the new connection referred to above. P.S. & V. of Lewisham published this early style card, probably about 1903 (a pencil message on the reverse is dated 1st Jan. 1905). As with the picture above, this is before the introduction of auto-trains on the branch and, indeed, the style of ballast suggests the picture could date from the 1890s. A recent view of the station at road level shows it occupied by an emporium known as Aladdin's Cave, although the sheets over the roof suggest it may not be in the best state of repair.

2873

This view of the end of the branch at Greenwich Park can be dated as between May 1912, when SE&CR Class 'P' 0-6-0T No. 325 was fitted for auto working on the line, and July 1914, when it was working on Otford to Sevenoaks and Westerham Branch trains. In to service in July 1910, the engine became No. 31325 under British Railways and was withdrawn in March 1960. This is an F. Moore card and shows us the generous accommodation provided at this now vanished terminus, which clearly failed to live up to expectations. Opened on 1st October 1888 as Greenwich ('Park' was added in 1900 on formation of the SE&CR), the station closed on 1st January 1917 and no trace of it remains, the site now buried beneath a hotel and car park. No doubt city gentleman did not appreciate the need to change trains at Nunhead, when there was another station a quarter of a mile away with the convenience of through services. The auto services were introduced as a last ditch attempt to save the line. Greenwich Park station comprised a substantial terminal building facing on to Stockwell Street, three platforms with covered accommodation, a centre release road and a short engine stabling siding. There were no goods facilities.

Catford station was but a short walk from the rival SER station at Catford Bridge – rival because this was an LC&DR station, who at the time were in competition with the SER. The walker in the right foreground is heading for Station Road, which will take him to the other station. The buildings this side of the bridge have been replaced by a modern entrance and booking office, while those on the other side have been totally cleared. The Shortlands & Nunhead Railway opened the station on 1st July 1892, that company being absorbed by the LC&DR in 1896. Station Road had changed its name to Adenmore Road by 1951.

Catford Station.

RIGHT: The LC&DR had another branch in south-east London, running from Nunhead to serve Crystal Palace. Opened in 1862, the line was electrified by the Southern Railway in 1925 but, in spite of this, patronage remained poor and deteriorated more when the Crystal Palace was destroyed in 1936. The line was closed for a couple of years during both wars and the damage it suffered during the second meant costly repairs were needed, so it closed from 20th September 1954. The station at Upper Sydenham, the last intermediate stop, was situated just south of Crescent Wood Tunnel, from which a train has just emerged behind 'A1' Class 0-4-4T No. 623. (originally LC&DR No. 164). Built in 1880, the engine was reboilered in 1908 (not obvious from the picture which dates from that period) and was the first of the class to be withdrawn, in June 1923. The card was clearly a sample being stamped on the back 'Gelatined' and handwritten 'Aquarelle'. A further rubber stamp gives the name of W. Dederich based at Ludgate Circus.

UPPER SYDENHAM STATION. S. E. & C. RLY.

S 5067   HIGH LEVEL STATION, CRYSTAL PALACE.

LEFT: The terminus of the branch was at Crystal Palace High Level station, quite a grand structure and clearly designed to fit in with the Crystal Palace which was adjacent and towered over it. 'A1' Class 0-4-4T No. 624 is ready to head for Victoria. Built as LC&DR No. 165 in 1880 and reboilered in 1908, the engine was withdrawn in September 1925. There were two further platforms through the arches on the right, hidden behind the display of advertising, which can only be described as extensive! Through the far end of the building the tracks curved round to an engine turntable. The wooden platforms remained till the end and note that the publishers of this card (WHS/Kingsway) had removed someone from the picture in the left foreground.

RIGHT: Jumping to the west, on another W.H. Smith's Kingsway card, we come to the line running from Brixton through Herne Hill and Penge. One of the intermediate stations on this line was Dulwich, which was opened by the LC&DR in October 1863. It is interesting to see that the station was referred to as West Dulwich on the card, which dates from before 1910, although the name was not officially changed until 20th September 1926. There is no sign of any motor traffic in this view, which is looking east along Thurlow Park Road, now part of the South Circular. The house agent today advertises Indian cuisine but the neat station building remains. The post box by the entrance has at some point been replaced by a pillar box on the pavement nearer to the road and the bridge span has been renewed, losing the iron support pillars.

S 7556   RAILWAY STATION, WEST DULWICH.

Communication is essential to the operation of a railway and this view shows some of what was needed, with an assortment of telegraph poles and wires. Space was clearly restricted here at Herne Hill, so the signal box was placed on a gantry straddling the running lines, which also carried the signals. These had semaphores for each direction on the same post, Distant signals only for Up trains to notify them of North Junction beyond the station, along with the Down Starters at the top of the posts. Note, too, that the Distant arms were still painted red with a white band at this date, the later and more commonly remembered yellow with black chevrons paint scheme coming in to use after 1918. The Down Starter signal on the left-hand post is in poor condition, a common problem at the time with wooden semaphore arms. The photographer was standing by the South Junction, where the lines for Tulse Hill (left) and Dulwich split. The view is looking north, with Herne Hill station – still recognisable today – visible in the background, beyond which was North Junction where the line split for Brixton (left) and Holborn Viaduct (right). All of these lines are still in operation today, making Herne Hill a busy location. Opened by the LC&DR on 25th August 1862, the view here was published by F. Moore around 1920 but the photograph is much older. The young lad sat of the railing outside the box is in railway uniform but the style of it and of the signalman leaning out of the window, coupled with the ash ballasted track, suggests a date possibly in the late 1890s. Through the signal box gantry, which lasted until 1956 when the box was replaced and demolished, can be seen the iron parapets of the bridge carrying the lines over Half Moon Lane.

RIGHT: Rarely captured on film on the suburban lines of South London were goods trains. Published by The Locomotive Publishing Company in 1904 or 1905, the picture was taken in August 1895 and shows a goods train passing the sidings at Herne Hill. The engine is one of the LC&DR's 'B' Class 0-6-0 goods engines, probably No. 138. Built in 1876, it is running with coal rails on the tender which were fitted circa 1893. Reboilered in 1902, it then ran as SE&CR No. 597 until withdrawn in October 1913. Two Midland railway open wagons stand to the left and the top of a private owner wagon can be seen beyond. The owners' name, Hockley Hall & Whately

Collieries & Brickworks Ltd, is clear to see – such wagons provided good mobile advertising for a company based in Tamworth, in Staffordshire. An industrial estate now covers the site of the old sorting sidings, which were on the Holborn Viaduct line between the railway and Milkwood Road.

ABOVE: Victoria was a complex station, with the termini for two railways, the LC&DR and the London Brighton & South Coast Railway, next to each other. This first view shows the interior of the LC&DR side, issued by the Libraire Continentale and captioned with the old railway name, although possibly published as late as 1910.

ABOVE: Dating from circa 1902, this early view by H.M.& Co. shows the large sign stressing the LC&DR's Continental connections. Behind it is the arched roof over the platforms, whilst to the right is the entrance to the Brighton side of the station, with the back of the Grosvenor Hotel beyond.

LEFT: This is a slightly later view of Victoria, published by Hartmann in 1903 or 1904, shortly before rebuilding commenced. The railway's name has been updated following the amalgamation of the SER and LC&DR and the different angle also allows the sign for Great Western Railway trains to be seen. The forecourt is jammed with cabs and a couple of buses, all still horse-drawn at this date.

Completed in 1906, the rebuilding of the SE&CR side of Victoria provided a much more imposing and befitting entrance. The railway's name featured high up above the entrance arch, while the GWR's services were still important enough for their name to appear a little lower down as well. Those more used to the segregation of London's termini following the 1923 Grouping will perhaps be surprised to see the name of the GWR featuring on this quintessentially Southern station (this is explained on page 140). Motor vehicles have now appeared on Wilton Road, with two omnibuses and a taxicab in the left foreground, and at least one more car visible in the distance. There is another smart looking motor parked in front of the station restaurant entrance but otherwise the cabs inside the station concourse are all still horse-drawn, as is also the bus on the right. Some work is underway just inside the gates and note the hut for British Cork Asphalt Ltd; registered in 1907 the company was short lived, the wind up order being issued on 16th January 1912. Like many of the general views that are contained within these pages, of the capital's major termini as generally seen by the travelling public and passers-by, the picture merits careful study. No one here was aware that the photographer was going about his business, capturing a moment in time for future generations to enjoy.

Victoria Station.

We now study the frontage of Victoria station from the west or Brighton side. The view, by Charles Martin, dates from about 1904 and the roof of the old South Eastern Railway part of the station that we have just been looking at is visible in the right background, behind the bulbous lamp. The LB&SCR building was rather more substantial than that of the SER, being a brick rather than a wooden structure. Beyond the horse-drawn omnibus is the large portico giving protection to passengers transferring to or from cabs, which can also be seen in the background of the previous pictures. A sign above it advertises cheap returns to Brighton every Sunday and Monday for 4 shillings and on the right is another board indicating that prospective visitors could book their tickets for the Crystal Palace, so that they did not have to queue on arrival. As was usually the case with Charles Martin's cards, there is much else to study in this view depicting turn-of-the-century Londoners going about their daily business.

RIGHT: We are now under the portico, which was decorated for a state visit by President Loubet of France on 6th July 1903, hence why this postcard was published by Neurdein Freres of Paris. The vertical lettering on the left indicates that it was printed from a stereotype (cliché) by C. Chusseau-Flaviens.

VOYAGE DU PRÉSIDENT LOUBET EN ANGLETERRE

(Cliché C. Chusseau-Flaviens)

7   6 Juillet 1903. — L'Arrivée à Victoria-Station, la Garde d'Honneur.   ND Phot

9
VICTORIA and LONDON BRIDGE
London, Brighton & South Coast Railway

ABOVE: As well as the LB&SCR's own trains, Victoria was the terminus for services from Willesden on the L&NWR, which were operated by that company. This train, for the 35 minute journey to Willesden, was a neat set of four 6-wheeled coaches, with guard's and luggage accommodation at each end; the second coach is First Class with four compartments compared to five in the one behind it. No. 816 was one of the 4ft 6in 2-4-2Ts dating from 1890. Allocated LM&SR No. 6589, the engine was withdrawn in September 1927 before it was applied.

LEFT: This unsigned F. Moore/Locomotive Publishing Co. card shows an unidentified 'Atlantic' at the outer end of what were very long platforms. The LB&SCR's side was constricted by the SER on one side and Buckingham Palace Road on the other, so the only way to expand was to lengthen the platforms to take two trains, with crossovers and, as here, an additional track to give access for and allow release of trains from the inner end.

A crowd of horse buses head off in all directions, whilst horse-drawn cabs line the road behind, with all of them having to negotiate the trestles of the temporary bridge that was used during the reconstruction of Victoria station, for bringing in materials and taking away rubbish without blocking the entrance. The new building is taking shape behind a forest of scaffolding. The reconstruction of the Brighton side was spread over a decade, between 1898 and 1908, whilst work on rebuilding the LC&DR's part of the station was all carried out in 1906. Although this postcard view of the rebuilding of the former was sent in November 1908, it is likely that it pre-dates the Charles Martin view a couple of pages earlier, as the sign above the portico is advertising cheap trains to Brighton on Sundays and Mondays for 3 shillings. There is also not a single motor vehicle to be seen amongst the melée here. On the horse buses, advertisements abound, with Nestlés milk chocolate, Pears soap and Colman's mustard being amongst the more familiar names that survived the test of time, and again there is much else to study here. Note for instance that many of the buses clearly worked to set routes, with their destinations painted on the boards that curl round with the rear-mounted steps up to the top deck.

Looking towards the footbridge and beyond the buffers, this view of Victoria shows how tracks were arranged to allow the necessary access when both ends of the platform were occupied. Clearly passengers needed to remember which train they were wanting to catch.

Battersea shed yard on a circa 1910 card by E. Pouteau, with little space to spare, the one line that is not occupied leading in to the roundhouses, so it had of course be kept clear. To the left we are looking over Queens Road (not visible) and into an area of Battersea Park that was known as The Wilderness.

Engines needed to be parked when not in use, maintained and prepared for the next turn of duty. The LB&SCR found space just across the river from Victoria at Battersea, where they built their depot for locomotives working into and out of the terminus. The covered sheds were built as roundhouses, where a central turntable provided access to the appropriate parking bay. A neat array of tank engines face on to the turntable here which, unlike those installed outdoors, was boarded over to prevent anyone falling in to the pit. From left to right, the locomotives on view are: Stroudley 'E' Class 0-6-0T No. 142 (*Toulon*), built in March 1879 and withdrawn in October 1950 as BR No. 32142, which here has a 'TANK EMPTY' circular notice on its chimney; Marsh 'I1' Class 4-4-2 'Atlantic' tank No. 1, which was new in June 1907, rebuilt to Class '11X' in December 1931 and withdrawn in July 1948; Billinton 'E4' Class 0-6-2T No. 471 (*Forest Hill*), built in June 1898 and withdrawn as BR No. 32471 in September 1959; Stroudley 'D1' Class 0-4-2T No. 277 (*Slinfold*), which entered traffic in December 1879 and was withdrawn in November 1926 without getting to wear the green livery of its new owners the Southern Railway, or be allocated a new number; and Billinton 'E5' Class 0-6-2T No. 574 (*Copthorne*), built in March 1903 and withdrawn as BR No. 32574 in June 1951. LB&SCR engines had usually been named (given here in brackets) but this policy was changed by Douglas Earle Marsh after his appointment as Locomotive, Carriage & Wagon Superintendent in November 1904. From the copper capped chimneys on No's 142 and 277, the engines seen here may be in the old livery and still carry names but the date of posting suggests that most will now be in the revised livery and nameless. Just visible on the right is a second roundhouse – there were three in total on the site. The area occupied by the locomotive sheds has been recently redeveloped and is now occupied by a number of apartment blocks. The anonymous card is one from an extensive correspondence to a young boy always referred to as 'Chum Dawson' and was posted in November 1910.

The busy station of Clapham Junction is actually situated, a little confusingly, in Battersea. Opened originally by the West London Extension Railway on 2nd March 1863, this unusual view of the station was taken during the rebuilding work carried out in 1908-09. The WLER was a joint construction involving four companies – the GWR, L&NWR, LB&SCR and the London & South Western Railway. The view is looking towards Waterloo from the L&SWR's Wimbledon Line platforms, on a postcard that was published anonymously. The platforms on the far right were for the LB&SCR's West End & Crystal Palace Line.

The headcode tells us that this was a day special heading from Victoria to Brighton, comprised mainly of Pullman carriages, the train having just passed through Clapham Junction. The card was not posted but the presence of the overhead electric wiring puts the date at 1911 or soon after, as this section came into use on 12th May 1911. Billinton 'B2' Class 4-4-0 No. 210 (previously named *Fairbairn*) was built in November 1897 and rebuilt to Class 'B2X' – the form seen here with larger boiler, shorter chimney and a more commodious cab – in February 1909. It was withdrawn in July 1931. The fine looking buildings in the background were the Royal Masonic Institution for Girls; the school relocated to Rickmansworth in 1934 (where it is still in operation today) and the site is now occupied by modern blocks of flats. The photograph was taken by Walter Bennett, whose work features in *The London, Brighton & South Coast Railway. The Bennett Collection* (Lightmoor Press 2011); however, much of this wonderful archive, as with this picture, is not properly dated.

S 7222   RAILWAY STATION, WANDSWORTH COMMON, LONDON.

RIGHT: The staff at Wandsworth Common station clearly had time to spare, to produce this fine flower display (pelargonium?) in the extensive station garden. Opened by the LB&SCR on 1st November 1869, the view here, once again on a W.H. Smith's Kingsway Series card, dates from about 1908, with no sign yet of the overhead electrification. Batchelar & Son, whose advertisement is prominent on the end of the main buildings on the Down side, were a removals and storage company, based in Croydon where they had a large depository.

RIGHT: The line coming from Clapham Junction passes through the common before running under Nightingale Lane and into Wandsworth Common station. The path seen here leading to the station runs across a small section of common from St. James's Drive. The path remains today, as do the buildings seen in these pictures, although the platform canopies have been cut back somewhat.

7696.   Wandsworth Common Station.   H.M&S.L.

Wandsworth Common Station   D.&M.349

LEFT: The headcode on the Down train heading though the station appears to be two plus signs, indicating that it was heading ultimately for West Croydon or Sutton. The LB&SCR system of headcodes was complex, with at least a hundred combinations in use. This photograph by D. & M. is a few years later than the previous platform view, as the overhead wiring for the electric service had been installed. The engine is Class 'D3' 0-4-4T No. 390 (originally named *St. Leonards*), built at Brighton in May 1894. Although displaced from London suburban services by electrification, many of the class continued to give service on country lines and this engine, as BR No. 32390, had the honour of being the last member in service when withdrawn in September 1955.

S 7292   BALHAM STATION.

Opened originally on 1st December 1856 but resited in 1863, Balham station was renamed Balham & Upper Tooting on 9th March 1927, which name it retained until 6th October 1969, after which it became plain Balham again. This W.H. Smith's Kingsway Series card would have been on sale at their bookstall on the left, where several racks of postcards can be seen amongst the books and magazines. However, under heavy enlargement those visible appear to be mostly studies of Edwardian theatre actresses, the popular beauties of the day. The gent standing in the classic 'I am important' pose so typical of the period could be the station master, although the pouch carried on a diagonal strap suggests he might be another official. The picture dates from about 1908, again predating electrification work, and is looking in the Down direction. Just past the end of the Down platform can be seen two of the low iron parapets of the bridge carrying the railway over Bedford Hill, beyond which it bifurcated at Balham Junction, the Croydon & Balham Line curving away to the south (right), whilst the Crystal Palace & West End Line carried straight on.

Balham Intermediate signal box was on the west side of the Croydon & Balham Line between Balham and Streatham Common stations, almost opposite the Tooting Bec swimming pool that had opened in the summer of 1906. The presence of the police and the military here was due to the first national railway strike that took place in 1911. The armed guard suggests a long dispute but in fact the official strike only lasted two days in August, although there had been unofficial action in the preceding days. The card was published anonymously.

Between Balham Intermediate signal box, just off picture to the right, and Bedford Hill bridge, which this time passed over the line, was a spot popular with photographers and some fine shots of moving trains were captured here. No. 219 was built as *Cleveland* in 1885 but was no longer named by the date of this circa 1912 view. Renumbered as No. 619 in December 1920, the engine survived for a further eight years. Note the Pullman Car third in the train. The card was another in The Locomotive Publishing Company's extensive series.

S 7236   STREATHAM HILL STATION & HIGH ROAD.

Returning to the Crystal Palace & West End Line, this fine mid-Edwardian view is looking north on Streatham Hill. LCC tramcar No. 814, approaching bound for Norbury, was again running on a system that utilised conduit current collection. Streatham Hill station features on the left of this WHS/Kingsway Series card, which is distinguished by a different lettering style to the other cards we have seen from this publisher. The covered dray and delivery cart both belong to the same private carrier but the picture is not clear enough to fully identify him. However, the lettering on the canvas indicates that they were prepared to make deliveries from 'STREATHAM HILL STATION TO ALL PARTS OF LONDON'. What is not clear from the picture is that the station building was constructed of timber and it is thus perhaps a little surprising to find that it is still in existence today. The buildings in the right distance also remain but the wooded area to the left was developed circa 1930. Note the Metropolitan Police Ambulance hut on the right, which probably housed a 2-wheeled, stretcher-bearing hand cart, facilitating the swift delivery of a patient to the nearest hospital.

After the scenes of industrial strife depicted at Balham, more normal times feature here at Streatham Hill signal box, with a relaxed looking signalman on the balcony, while a track worker stands on the steps. Note the railed balcony round the building to enable safe access for window cleaning; it was important to ensure good visibility, as the signalman had to record all passing trains. The box was on the south side of the line to the west of the station and also controlled access to a coal depot on the opposite side of the line, plus an extensive bank of carriage sidings, which were just out of sight on the right in this view. A large carriage shed was later built covering these, probably during the Second World War, as it does not feature on a 1938 OS map but is there by 1949. Rebuilt in 2010, the site is today in use as Streatham Hill Traincare Depot.

The station at Tulse Hill was opened by the LB&SCR on 1st October 1868, with the LC&DR arriving the following year. Another Charles Martin published card, dating from around 1904 and full of interest as usual, this is Approach Road, which led from Norwood Road to the station entrance. This was on the west side of the line and the road remains today but has been named Station Rise. We are used to station names appearing on lamps but here we have the main road – NORWOOD R^D – featuring in the lamp glass on the left. Apart from the horse-drawn transport, the scene is remarkably little changed today and even the pub remains, as The White Hart; slightly oddly, no name is visible anywhere here but it may well have been The White Hart then. Note the offices of Rickett, Smith & Co. on the left, coal & coke merchants who were a large south London based concern with their own fleet of wagons.

There are a considerable number of south London stations with Hill in their name and this view of Gipsy Hill gives a clue as to why. Posted but with an illegible date, this Kingsway card dates as usual from about 1908. Opened on 1st December 1856 and provided with the neat building seen here, the station was officially Gipsy Hill for Upper Norwood until British Railways dropped the Upper Norwood reference. The view looking north on Gipsy Hill Road is little changed today. A parcels dray waits in front of the station and the array of coal merhcants offices just beyond it include Moger & Co. Ltd, H. Wilsher & Co. and Rickett, Smith & Co.

S 7300   GIPSY HILL STATION L. B. & S.C. RAILY.

Forest Hill Station.

The London & Greenwich Railway was one of the first lines to be built in London and they opened Dartmouth Arms station here on 5th of June 1839, which was named after the nearby Dartmouth Arms Inn. It was given the more familiar name of Forest Hill from 3rd July 1845. The station is often referred to as Forest Hill for Lordship Lane and should not be confused with the station on the Crystal Palace High Level Branch known as Lordship Lane for Forest Hill. Four tracks run through the station but today the central island platform has gone and only the outer lines have platforms. The rest of the station has been completely modernised and the scene is virtually unrecognisable today, the old buildings seen here having suffered during the Second World War, whilst the road in the foreground is again now part of the South Circular. The emporiums surrounding the station include the seemingly obligatory florists shop, in front of which stands a London B-Type omnibus. The bus is lettered Metropolitan, the fleet name used by the MET Omnibus Co. from 1920, whilst the card was sent on 18th July 1924, so the view is within that date range. Registration No. LF9676, the white AK18 board on the side of the bus just behind the driver's seat indicates that it was allocated to Streatham depot and was operating Route 49, from Shepherds Bush to Steatham Common.

Unlike the locomotive shed at Battersea where roundhouses were used, the depot at New Cross had two straight buildings, one of three roads and one of four. It was a skilled job, the responsibility of the shed foreman, just to make sure that every engine was in the right position to get out for the next duty. Published by the Locomotive Publishing Company in 1905, the picture dates from about 1900, at which period LB&SCR locomotives all still carried names. On the left, 'D3' Class 0-4-4T No. 396 *Clayton* stands adjacent to a small stage used when coaling, although coal would have been lifted up by the steam crane alongside. In the centre, one of Billinton's 'E5' Class 0-6-2 tanks – sadly the name is not quite readable but the engine would be quite new at this date – stands back to back with a 'D' Class 0-4-2T over the ash pit, used to rake out the ash that would collect in the firebox. There was much hard work involved with this, firstly working under the engine to rake the ash out and then later clearing it from the pit, loading into a wagon for disposal. The batch of engines on the right include 'C' Class 0-6-0T No. 451 *Helvetia*, behind which is 'D3' Class 0-4-4T No. 373 *Billingshurst*, with 'B2' Class 4-4-0 No. 322 *G.P. Bidder* to its right. Of the engines that we can positively identify, all were built in the 1890s. Today on this site you would be looking at a supermarket.

DEPTFORD "LIFT" BRIDGE OVER THE GRAND SURREY CANAL.   Waterlow & Sons Ltd.

ABOVE: We are now looking south in this wider view, with New Cross Gate station to the left and the shed, seen from the opposite end, on the right. Note the signal box in the centre squeezed in between the tracks. 'Gate' was only added to the name in 1923, until which time there had been two stations named New Cross – this one on the London & Croydon, with the other on the South Eastern Railway.

LEFT: Just north of New Cross station, the LB&SCR had a branch leading to the Thames at Deptford Wharf. En route, the line had to cross the Grand Surrey Canal and of course barges had to be allowed access. To give the necessary clearance a lift bridge was constructed with enough clearance for the limited height of the barges. The railway company included this view in Set 5 of their official postcards, which depicted a number of interesting bridges on their lines. The signal box in the background is Bricklayers Arms Junction. LBSC-019

RIGHT: Opened on 1st December 1865, Denmark Hill station was on the LB&SCR's South London Line, running between Victoria and London Bridge. The station was also served by SE&CR Crystal Palace trains and Greenwich Park services. These ran from Victoria and from Moorgate, and there were also trains from St. Paul's to Catford and Orpington. The very fine building seen here still survives, although it was damaged by fire in 1980 but has been renovated and now operates as The Phoenix. The entrance was as seen here on Windsor Road, which was off Champion Park but is now on the latter road. To the right of the lads with their barrow is a notice with Hackney Carriage information, while the sign above states 'STANDING FOR THREE HACKNEY CARRIAGES'. The station also had a Public Telephone Call Office. Posted in 1906, the card was published by the Card House, 84 Rye Lane, S.E.

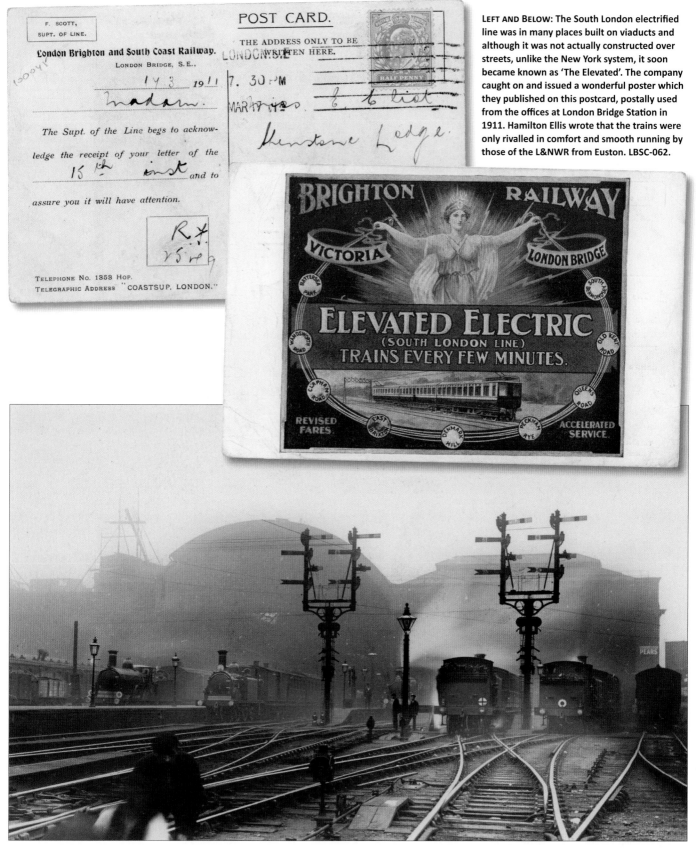

F. SCOTT,
SUPT. OF LINE.

London Brighton and South Coast Railway.

LONDON BRIDGE, S.E.,

14 3 19 11

madam.

The Supt. of the Line begs to acknowledge the receipt of your letter of the
15 th inst and to
assure you it will have attention.

R *
r5 reg

TELEPHONE No. 1858 HOP.
TELEGRAPHIC ADDRESS "COASTSUP, LONDON."

POST CARD.

THE ADDRESS ONLY TO BE
WRITTEN HERE.

LONDON.S.E

HALF PENNY

7. 30 PM
MAR 17 11. E. 6 tiet

Kenstone Ledge.

LEFT AND BELOW: The South London electrified
line was in many places built on viaducts and
although it was not actually constructed over
streets, unlike the New York system, it soon
became known as 'The Elevated'. The company
caught on and issued a wonderful poster which
they published on this postcard, postally used
from the offices at London Bridge Station in
1911. Hamilton Ellis wrote that the trains were
only rivalled in comfort and smooth running by
those of the L&NWR from Euston. LBSC-062.

BRIGHTON RAILWAY
VICTORIA   LONDON BRIDGE
ELEVATED ELECTRIC
(SOUTH LONDON LINE)
TRAINS EVERY FEW MINUTES.
REVISED FARES   ACCELERATED SERVICE.

We began this tour of the LB&SCR lines from Victoria station, so now it is time to return to central London, to visit the company's terminus platforms at
London Bridge station. Every locomotive in this busy scene carries a different headcode, in what could be a line-up waiting for the start of the rush hour
commute, with five trains waiting to head south. Note too that once again each post of the bracket signals carries arms for both Up and Down trains. None
of the engines are positively identified but the two on the left are headed by a 'Gladstone' Class 2-4-0 and a 'D' Class tank engine respectively. The scene
has dramatically changed today with the rebuilding of the station and the Shard now towering above it but even in this circa 1905 anonymously published
view there is construction work in progress in the left background.

LONDON BRIDGE STATION.

LEFT: From Raphael Tuck's 'London Railway Stations' Series II, this lovely coloured view of London Bridge shows a train that has just arrived from the South Coast behind 'B4' Class 4-4-0 No. 71 *Goodwood*. Built in September 1901, the engine was rebuilt to Class 'B4X' in June 1923 and lasted in service until October 1951, when it was withdrawn as BR No. 32071, although it apparently still carried Southern Railway lettering on its tender. The luggage being pushed along by the porter is typical of what would be taken at this period for just a few days away from home.

BELOW: Published by LL about 1908, this view features an impressive line-up of horse-drawn omnibuses and a few cabs outside London Bridge station. Note the leg protectors worn by the drivers.

165   LONDON. — London Bridge Station.   LL.

LEFT: With a time table for the South London Line on display on the right, it is thought this scene must be at either London Bridge or Victoria but this is yet to be confirmed. The men stand proudly with their Shand Mason fire engine which, although somewhat obscured, appears to be a hand pump. Lettered for the railway company, it also carries a very stylish number 7 in the centre and presumably the men were also LB&SCR employees, although no insignia can be identified to confirm this. You could buy chocolate from the slot machine just visible in the right background and then check your weight on the scales to the left. It is interesting to see the Brighton poster just above the man's head on the left, as this was also on a postcard (Ref. LBSC-063), the example seen being used by the company to acknowledge correspondence and posted in March 1908. This would give a probable date for this anonymous unused card of 1906 or 1907.

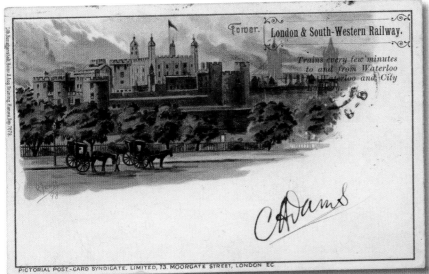

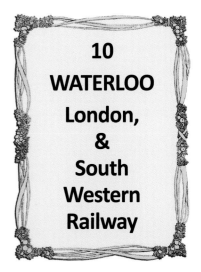

10
WATERLOO
London, & South Western Railway

ABOVE: Sent to an address in Holland in 1899, this is another of the cards sold from slot machines, again featuring a lovely picture by R. Joust, dated 1898, showing the Tower of London with Tower Bridge in the background. Printed for the London & South Western Railway, the card advertises the Waterloo & City Railway (commonly known as 'The Drain') which was opened in 1898. Card reference is LSW-803.

RIGHT: Whilst heading probably for Nine Elms (for which it is lettered), this covered dray ran into difficulties while trying to operate during the strike of August 1911. It is seen here at an unknown location being reloaded with boxes apparently filled with meat, after being overturned by strike supporters.

The photo shows a railway van which was overturned while conveying goods to our warehouse, during the great London Strike Aug. 10th. 1911.

LEFT: A local train stands in Platform 1 at Waterloo station, Central section, behind one of the Adams 4-4-2Ts, known as 'Radial Tanks'. This is a Tuck card from Series 9279, which was published in March 1906 and whilst it does look as though the local is in Platform 2, there was just a single line for Platform 1, so rather confusingly it thus had platform faces both sides. Some good period fashions are also on show here and note the lad on the right selling newspapers. No longer in use at this date, the central of the three lines in the foreground (the near platform hides the third) led to an erstwhile bridge taking a connecting line across the road to the SE&CR.

RIGHT: This card by J. Beagles & Co. Ltd was not sent, so there is no postmark to assist with dating it but changes in fashion from the previous postcard suggest the picture was taken some time between 1910 and the Great War. This expansive general view only shows a part of the concourse, that serving Platforms 3, 4, 5 and 6, and includes three W.H. Smith's bookstalls as well.

BELOW: This is actually a fairly quiet scene at Waterloo, with the train in Platform 4 having been in long enough for all of the passengers to have gone. However, there are plenty of cabs waiting for the next arrival, when doubtless it would seem that chaos had descended again. On the left, several luggage porters have time to chat alongside the now empty parcels coach. The card, by Wrench, dates from 1903 or 1904 and shows the view from the footbridge.

547.Z. **WATERLOO STATION, LONDON.** BEAGLES' POSTCARDS.
THIS BUSY STATION IS THE TERMINUS FOR THE LONDON & SOUTH WESTERN RAILWAY, WHICH SERVES THE SOUTH-WESTERN PART OF ENGLAND AND THE PORTS OF EMBARKATION FOR THE CONTINENT AND ABROAD.

OPPOSITE PAGE TOP: G.W. Secretan of Tufnell Park was responsible for this photographic postcard where the many troops in evidence suggest a First World War view. One soldier in the centre has a bugle across his back and the man next to him appears to be holding a similar instrument but there is otherwise no information given to assist us as to the occasion. If it is the 1914-18 war period, the guess is from the number of well-dressed onlookers to be seen that it shows troops embarking for, rather than returning from, France.

London.
The Wrench Series, No. 7981
Waterloo Station, Interior.

RIGHT: Looking out along Platform 1, showing the single line running in between it and Platform 2, on the right, as mentioned on the previous page. A train has just arrived at the latter and has disgorged a a crowd of passengers who now head for the barrier. The left hand face of Platform 2 did not have a number, although passengers could disembark on either side from a train arriving in on the single track. The light construction of the original roof is clearly shown in both of these views. The card, again dating from circa 1903, was published anonymously and whilst it looks very similar in style to the Wrench card above, this was probably a result of it having been produced by the same printing works.

Waterloo Station (Interior). *London.*

Part of an extensive correspondence between J. Harold Wright of Bingley in Yorkshire and A.J. Blanchet of Richmond in Surrey, this card was sent to the latter in June 1905. Looking out along Platforms 2 and 3, it clearly shows the centre line that lead to the bridge to the SE&CR, apparently out of use with a block placed across the track. Note the stylish platform indicator board on the left and the 'ghosts' on the platform caused by the long time exposure required.

A view from around 1910 of the outer end of the platforms, showing one of the narrow wooden extensions that were squeezed into the tightest space possible – not something that would be countenanced in this day and age, although the lack of space at Waterloo is still an issue. Drummond 'T9' Class 4-4-0 No. 716, seen here at the head of a train for Southampton, was built by Dübs & Co. in 1899. Fleet of foot, these stylish engines quickly earned the nickname 'Greyhounds' and all of the sixty-six strong class were equipped with superheating in the 1920s, No. 716 in 1927, improving their abilities even further. As No. 30716, the engine was an early withdrawal for the class by BR, in October 1951. The card was published anonymously.

Another card from the Wright/ Blanchet correspondence, posted on 23rd December 1904 but this time from Richmond to Bingley, this presents a rather different view of Waterloo. In fact we are looking at 'The Drain', the Waterloo & City line which was opened on 11th July 1898, the picture probably being taken just before that date. Constructed for the L&SWR by John Mowlem & Co., with all electric traction equipment supplied by Siemens & Co. and with electrically operated signals (apart from a few semaphores in the open at the Waterloo end) from Sykes & Co., at the time it opened it was the only part of Waterloo station that was electrified.

RIGHT: Following on from the title page spread of the old and new boxes at Waterloo, this photograph shows the inside of the earlier cabin, with the photographer able to get a clear view. Note the gas lamps; on the one in front of the track diagram it is just possible to make out the loop at the end of a chain, which would have been one of a pair attached to an arm controlling the gas. A pole with a hook would be used to pull the appropriate end down to turn gas on or off and a pilot flame would ignite the lamp when gas was turned on. There was also a stove to provide some heating. The anonymous card dates from around 1905 but the picture was probably taken just after closure in 1889, hence the lack of staff. The stylish art nouveau lady on the far right was perhaps a nod to another popular postcard collecting theme of the day but she otherwise looks incongruously out of place.

RIGHT: Staff pose for the photographer in this 1920 view inside the later Waterloo 'A' box, which was electrically lit by this date. The comparison between this and the earlier picture above is interesting, spotting the changes brought about by progress.

Vauxhall Station Wandsworth Road.

LEFT: Vauxhall Bridge station was opened by the L&SWR on 11th July 1848, taking its name from the nearby bridge over the Thames but it became simply Vauxhall in 1862. Today Vauxhall Bridge carries the A205 road, which then passes under the railway through the span just behind the horse tram. The buildings on the left have gone but those on the railway side of this view look much the same today. There is now a footbridge over the A205 that appears to be hung from the railway bridge and the windows are hidden behind hoardings. This is a Charles Martin card posted in November 1905 with the picture a year or so earlier. Did the signal on the roof of the pub on the left serve a railway purpose?

RIGHT: The Card House were the publishers of this exterior view captioned 'Nine Elms Station', which was posted in June 1910. Used as offices for many years, this was the original terminus of the L&SWR, opened on 21st May 1838. The only attraction nearby was the Vauxhall Pleasure Gardens, which appear to have been losing their appeal at that time, whilst it was not exactly convenient for passengers having to transfer to boat or carriage to reach central London, so the railway quickly extended the line to Waterloo. This by-passed Nine Elms station, which closed to passengers on 11th July 1848. Sadly this original building, designed by Sir William Tite, was demolished about 1960 and there is no longer any railway on the north side of the main line. The goods depot closed in July 1968 and much of the site is now occupied by the New Covent Garden Market.

RIGHT BELOW: The offices and clock tower at Nine Elms stood between two turntables serving what was the second shed, built in the form of a semi-roundhouse. Maintenance work was in hand but of course all stopped for the photographer. The postcard dates from about 1905 but the picture could be a couple of years earlier. There are tender locomotives on view here but in the last few years before demolition in 1909, this part of the shed was only used for tank engines.

BELOW: Dating from the late 1880s, this turntable served a new straight shed and was of 50ft diameter rather than the pair of 42ft turntables serving the roundhouse. Engines continued to increase in size and this was in turn replaced by a 65ft turntable about 1910. The engine, 'M7' Class No. 669, was built in September 1897 and lasted until July 1961. Locomotives of this class were still to be seen at Waterloo on empty stock duties until the end of the 1950s.

There was a lot of effort put into the appearance of pre-Grouping locomotives, partly because they acted as advertisements for their respective companies but also perhaps from a competitive point of view in areas where various of the different railways rubbed up against each other. London was the ultimate example of this, with nine of the major railways plus several other smaller companies being represented, so there is no doubt that the cleaners posing here would have been justifiably pleased with the gleaming 'T1' Class 0-4-4 tank engine they have just finished working on, standing outside the Nine Elms roundhouse. As can just be discerned from the small lettering round the edge of the oval numberplate, No. 11 was built at Nine Elms Works in June 1895. It was withdrawn by the Southern Railway in April 1944. Cleaner was the lowest rung on the ladder for lads wishing to become footplate crew, so those seen here would almost certainly have worked their way up to become firemen in due course and later probably drivers as well. However, one or two of them may also have gone off to fight in the war; many felt it was their duty to do so, although footplate crew were under no obligation to volunteer for service.

RIGHT: Some simple accommodation was provided by the turntable at Nine Elms, where in about 1905 a number of workers dutifully pose. To the left is an end view of the coaling stage that dated from the late 1880s, with a coal wagon inside which would have been shunted up an incline at the far end.

BELOW: Cranes are an essential piece of railway equipment. This Stothert & Pitt steam crane, built at their works in Bath in 1908, was allocated to Nine Elms, where it was photographed probably soon after delivery. It looks to have fixed wheels under the boiler and a bogie to allow it to negotiate sharp curves, either side of which there is a jack that could be screwed down to provide greater stability when the crane was working. The coaling stage, seen again behind, had been re-roofed circa 1900 and was finally replaced in 1923.

ABOVE: The scene in the Machine Shop at Nine Elms Works about 1905. With the machines all driven by belts from an overhead system and metal being worked on continuously, just imagine the racket when all was operating!

BELOW: A similar view of organised chaos inside the Wheel Shop, on a card posted in April 1907. Note that the roof let in plenty of light.

The original Nine Elms Works were situated on the north side of the line but this restricted site near the old passenger station was soon found to be inadequate. Accordingly, a new works was constructed on the opposite side of the line, close to the engine shed, which came into use in the 1860s. The locomotives seen under construction here are 'G14' Class 4-6-0s (No's 453-457), that were built at Nine Elms in the spring of 1908. As with all these views of the shed and works, the card was published anonymously but the photograph is known to have been taken by J.B. Ashford, on 14th March 1908 (see *LSWR Locomotives, The Drummond Classes* by D.L. Bradley, Wild Swan 1986, p128) so perhaps he was responsible for some of the other pictures as well. The 'G14's were amongst the last new engines to be constructed at Nine Elms Works before it too closed with the opening of Eastleigh Works in 1909. The narrow gauge rails seen here and in the view of the Machine Shop were for 4-wheeled trolleys on which heavy tools or components could be loaded to move them around the works more easily. Smaller items could be taken on 2-wheeled barrows with a basket on the front, as demonstrated by the one partly in view in the right foreground; a fuller version of the image appears in the above mentioned volume.

LEFT: The L&SWR Loco Works Brass Band posed outside the west end of the Boiler Shop at Nine Elms in 1907. The wording on the caps is not clear, certainly 'L S W R' at the top and then possibly 'Loco Works' underneath. The elderly bearded gentleman sat in the centre is Dugald Drummond, L&SWR Chief Mechanical Engineer from 1895 until his death in 1912, who was aged 67 at the time of this picture. He was responsible for the design and construction of several very successful classes of locomotives for the company during his time in office, such as the 'T9' 4-4-0s and the 'M7' 0-4-4Ts. The man on his left, behind the large drum and wearing a braided uniform that differs from everyone else's attire, was presumably the bandmaster.

RIGHT: A final rather sad view of Nine Elms Works in 1913, with demolition well under way after all of the machinery had been stripped out.

LEFT: Clapham Junction North signal box gives us another look at how the authorities reacted to the strike in 1911 with both police and military on duty protecting the men in the box, who were effectively strikebreakers. One may well wonder at the suitability of the bearskin helmets when on active duty. Despite its name, the box is thought to have been on the south side of the line at Clapham, to the north-east of the platforms and near where Falcon Road ran beneath the railway.

This general view looking to the west at Clapham Junction was taken in August 1907. On the right are the Windsor lines, with carriage sidings in the centre of the picture. To the left of these an L&SWR train is coming through the Wimbledon line platforms and there are more platforms for the LB&SCR line – which we have already explored – to the left again. Finally, on the far left edge of the photograph are the platforms of the West London Extension Railway for trains, heading north across the river towards Olympia and Willesden Junction. The work of rebuilding Clapham Junction station was spread over a number of year, as indicated by the view of reconstruction underway on the LB&SCR side in 1908-09 on page 101. Here, a year or so earlier, building work on the L&SWR's Windsor lines side of the station is seen in progress, with the newly built Clapham Junction East (later 'A') signal box straddling two tracks one of which was still being laid; for reasons that are not clear, the box did not come in to operation until 1912. Rebuilt and enlarged piecemeal over the years, Clapham Junction East (later 'A') signal box finally closed on 25th May 1990. It is thought that the box seen in the previous view, Clapham Junction North, was sited just off picture to the left. Apart from the loss of the box and the addition of third rail electrification, much of this scene would still be recognisable today, with a multiple unit maintenance depot now occupying the carriage sidings, whilst the long footbridge linking all of the platforms still in place.

LEFT: E.& C.'s Up-to-Date Series of postcards included this coloured view of Clapham Junction, dating from about 1905 and produced from an original photograph by R.W. Thomas. The engine is No. 648, one of the Adams 'A12' Class 0-4-2s; also known as 'Jubilees', they proved to be equally at home on goods or passenger services. Built at Nine Elms in November 1894, No. 648 was in service until July 1947. The view shows the stylish buildings on the Wimbledon line side of the station, which were soon to be replaced, with the LB&SCR platforms in the right foreground.

RIGHT: A last look at the 1911 strike as it affected the lines of the main line companies shows two more bearskin wearing soldiers guarding signals in Clapham Cutting. The little hut was not for their benefit but was provided for a fog signalman, who would be responsible for placing detonators on the track to indicate a signal at danger in poor visibility. This postcard is also an example of one of the pitfalls occasionally encountered when attempting to date a picture, being printed on the reverse with post regulations that were superseded in 1907. However, the scene is clearly 1911, so no problem this time, the card being an example almost certainly of a photographer using up old paper stock.

3169

EARLSFIELD:— THE RAILWAY STATION

LEFT: The first station beyond Clapham Junction was Earlsfield, opened on 1st April 1884 as Earlsfield & Summer Town, the latter name bing dropped from 1st June 1902. The opening of the station probably tied in with the widening of the line from two to four tracks, with housing in the area expanding rapidly in the latter part of the 19th century. A passenger train approaches behind 'L12' Class 4-4-0 No. 417, which came into service in June 1904 and survived with various modifications over the years to be withdrawn by BR in October 1951. The card is numbered 3169 but has no publishers name; it was used in November 1908.

An express from Waterloo approaches Durnsford Road Bridge, just on the London side of Wimbledon. The engine is 'L12' No. 417 again, which was stationed at Bournemouth when new and is probably heading there in this view. This postcard dates from about 1908 and shows a siding heading off across the fields on the left, which served an oil gas works. On the right is another siding which ran to the Wimbledon Borough Council Electricity Works. The area on the left was later covered over with carriage sidings and also by Durnsford Road power station, which was built for the electric trains. The siding to the electricity works appears to have fallen out of use in the early 1950s and the works closed in 1968.

WIMBLEDON: RAILWAY FROM DURNSFORD ROAD BRIDGE.   P. 1257.

TOOTING JUNCTION   J.335.

A rare view of the original V-shaped Tooting Junction station, which opened on 1st October 1868. Closure came about on 12th August 1894, when a replacement was brought in to use a little to the west. The main building of the new station can be seen in the distance on the bridge, with the platforms visible through the span. Both sides of the junction were lines coming in from Wimbledon, that on the left via Haydons Road, the other via Merton Abbey. Both were also part of the Tooting, Merton & Wimbledon Railway, which was jointly operated by the LB&SCR and L&SWR. The route on the right had only the one intermediate station at Merton Abbey and suffered from the competion provided first by road transport and then from the underground when the Northern Line was extended to Morden. Consequently, it closed to passengers from 3rd March 1929, after previously losing its services between 31st December 1916 and 27th August 1923 due to the war. The goods yard and shed, just in view on the right, remained in use, with goods traffic continuing until 5th August 1968 (and until 1st May 1975 to a coal depot at Merton Abbey). However, it was served from Wimbledon, the junction here being severed on 10th March 1934. The old station building on the left here appears to be in private use, with the edge of the platform protected by a fence. It survived until the late 20th century but its site is now hidden beneath a block of flats, whilst a supermarket now occupies the platforms and goods yard on the right, with the twin tracks still running through to Tooting station in the background. The card was published by Johns and posted in September 1912.

RIGHT: Dating from around 1908, this card shows the second Tooting Junction station, which opened on 12th August 1894, replacing the original seen in the previous picture situated just 300 yards away. Travelling eastwards, the electric tram is working from overhead current collection and just look at the wall of advertising behind it. The station, on the west side of London Road (now the A217), looks much the same today, the entrance and ticket office building on the left being still in use. Indeed most if not all of the buildings in this picture still survive, although the wall is now hidden by a new house built just the other side of the station entrance. 'Junction' was dropped from the station name in 1938. The signals seemingly protruding from the roof were on a bracket shown in the first view, set high up so they could be seen against a sky background by the footplate crews of Up trains.

LEFT: Heading back northwards from Tooting Junction but on the other line (the one still open today) we reach the Tooting, Merton & Wimbledon station at Haydons Road, which was opened as Haydons Lane on 1st October 1868. 'Lane' was changed to 'Road' from 1st October 1889, no doubt reflecting an upgrading of the thoroughfare on which the station was situated. The view is looking east and the track will start to curve south in the distance towards Tooting Junction. The station is still open today and the buildings seen here survived until the early 1990s, when they were replaced by bus shelters and a new red brick ticket office at the time adjacent land was developed for housing.

RIGHT: There is now a bit of a jump for us to reach the final two L&SWR stations to be visited, for they are situated north of the River Thames. The first, Chiswick & Grove Park, is near Barnes Bridge, on the Hounslow loop line. The station was opened as Chiswick on 22nd August 1849 by the Windsor, Staines & South Western Railway, a company formed in 1847 to extend the Richmond Railway of 1846. The latter was absorbed by the L&SWR soon after it opened and the WS&SWR quickly followed suit. '& Grove Park' was added to the name on 1st November 1872 but was dropped again in December 1920, whilst some pictures show 'For Grove Park' on the station nameboard. This is the view east from the station footbridge, looking along a sylvan Burlington Lane on the left. The station is still open and the classic main building remains but is now a private house. The smaller building is now the ticket office but the goods shed behind has gone.

CHURCHFIELD ROAD & NORTH LONDON RAILWAY STATION, ACTON.

APPLEBY SERIES, 12 CHURCHFIELD RD. ACTON.

The view looking east along Churchfield Road in Acton in around 1908 is a scene still easily recognised today. On the left is part of Acton signal box, now long gone, whilst the gates have inevitably been replaced by automatic lifting barriers. The end of the station building on the right now houses a café and there are still plenty of trees beyond the level crossing. The station was opened on 1st August 1853 as Acton, becoming Acton Central on 1st November 1925. This was a part of the North & South Western Junction Railway, which had just 5½ route miles running southwards from Willesden Junction. Services were operated by the North London Railway, although the line was leased jointly to the L&NWR and the L&SWR until 1871, when the NLR became partners too. However, the N&SWJR remained independent until the 1923 Grouping, when it became a part of the London, Midland & Scottish Railway. Along with the rest of the North London route, the line was threatened with closure in the 1960s but, happily, this was averted and today the station is served by the Stratford to Richmond service of London Overground. It is now the point of change from overhead to third rail current supply. The original main building survives as the Station House pub and retains the look of a station; although not listed, the building does have local protection.

11
PADDINGTON
Great
Western
Railway

ABOVE: Just occasionally advertisements give a good indication of the picture date and here, in the right foreground, there is a poster for the Windsor Races on Friday July 22nd and Saturday July 23rd 1904. The view is looking west along Praed Street with the Great Western Royal Hotel (the card title does not use the 'Royal') on the right. The hotel was opened in 1854 but the GWR leased it to a subsidiary until 1896, the Great Western Royal Hotel Company, of which Brunel was the first chairman, the hotel having been his idea. Enlarged in the 1936-38 period, it ceased to be a railway hotel when it was sold in 1983 and today it is one of the Hilton chain of hotels. Regrettably, 'Great Western Royal' has been dropped from the name, so losing the historical reference.

RIGHT: Series 1 of the Great Western Railway's officially issued postcards came out in April 1904, and they were proud to include this view of the Royal Waiting Room at Paddington station. Provided originally for Queen Victoria, this would have constituted a comfortable resting point between the carriage from Buckingham Palace and the train to Windsor. Queen Victoria was a regular traveller by train, her first journey being with the GWR on 13th June 1842, behind a locomotive driven by Daniel Gooch; Isambard Kingdom Brunel was also on the footplate. The need to travel between her various residences and to make Royal visits led to most of the larger pre-Grouping railway companies building special carriages for her to ride in, leading, by the end of the 19th century, to the construction of full Royal trains. Situated on Platform 1, the Royal Waiting Room has today been adapted for use as a First Class Waiting Room. Reference GW004, the card is from the first issue of the set, which comprised twenty-five cards, sold for a shilling the set or two for a penny from a slot machine.

LEFT: This view of Paddington was included by Raphael Tuck in Series 9279 'London Railway Stations'. It provides a good view into the cab of a 2-4-0 that would have run in tender first with the empty coaches for the express that is just loading. After the departure of this, it would then probably be taking a shorter distance stopping train out as its next duty. On the right, a 4-4-0 has brought an express into Platform 8, one of the main arrival platforms conveniently situated next to the cab road. On the left, having just brought in a local service, is a 'Metro' 2-4-0 tank, with open cab and fitted with condensing apparatus for working the Metropolitan lines

36650. London. Paddington Station Arrival Platforms. C.N.

ABOVE: Another of the superb Photochrom published photographs by Carl Norman shows us the opposite view on Platform 8 circa 1904, with a double line of cabs on the cab road. Beyond the end of the arched roof this road led up by the hotel to emerge on to Praed Street.

BELOW: Again by Carl Norman and looking towards the buffers is this lovely view over departure Platforms 3 to 7, which shows to advantage Brunel's splendid roof. There is also a great deal of detail to be seen on the carriage roofs, which are all clerestory style. Note particularly the steam railmotor by the buffers on Platform 5. Pictures of these vehicles in the station are unusual and it seems they only worked into the terminus on Sundays; weekdays saw them stop at Westbourne Park because of congestion at Paddington.

36649. London. Paddington Station. Departure Platforms. C.N.

The previous two pictures having been rather quiet, here is a rather different scene published by Wymans about 1912 and showing the main departure Platforms 1 and 2. From the number of boaters to be seen, it has to be summer holiday time.

At the outer end of the station, a local is just departing behind 2-4-0 No. 3241 in an otherwise quiet scene. A member of the '3232' Class built at Swindon in November 1892, the engine was withdrawn in April 1927. It looks to be fitted with an S4 type boiler, which it was rebuilt with in October 1905. Built originally as express engines, they had been superseded by larger more powerful locomotives by the end of the century and were subsequently relegated to local and branch line services. Those stationed in the London area also regularly worked on the milk trains. They did not have numberplates, the brass numerals being mounted directly on the rear splasher in an arc. The card is one published by E. Pouteau circa 1907.

From much the same viewpoint as the previous picture, 4-4-0 No. 3701 *Stanley Baldwin* is seen just starting out at the head of a local train. This coloured picture was produced by painting over a photograph and it was done with great accuracy by F. Moore, although he 'repaired' a broken pane on the end of the façade. No. 3701 was a member of the 'Bulldog' Class, built in April 1906 but not named until January 1909, with the picture probably dating from that year. The engine cost £1,910, and was in service until November 1938, having become No. 3411 in 1912, whilst its name was removed in 1937, when 'Castle' Class 4-6-0 No. 5063 *Thornbury Castle* was renamed *Earl Baldwin* a month after entering service.

Looking a little elderly here is 'Chancellor' Class 2-4-0 No. 154, as it heads the 12.30pm train to Birmingham beneath Bishops Bridge Road. For accounting purposes No. 154 was classified as renewal of an earlier engine (in other words a virtually new build), entering service in November 1878. It was the only one of the class to carry a name, being named *Chancellor* in honour of a visit to Wolverhampton Works by the Chancellor of the Exchequer Sir William Harcourt whilst the engine was being built. Reboilered on four occasions, No. 154 was withdrawn in May 1919. The man on the track looks as though he has a brazier burning close by, suggesting this is a winter scene. This is a Pouteau card of unknown date but pre-1910.

RIGHT: Published by R.E. Dukes of Islington, this is a picture that may not appeal to everybody but is nevertheless an interesting piece of social history. It is odd that there is no mention of what the dog was collecting money for but it would have been a railwayman's charity, such as an orphanage. Stuffed and mounted, even after death he was able to continue collecting – note the slot for coins in the bottom of the frame. When alive Tim was apparently allowed to run free on to Royal trains and could nose out the important person to receive a contribution.

BELOW: The Besses-o'-th'-Barn Brass Band, from Bury, is still going and now rapidly approaching its two hundredth anniversary. They won the National Competition at Crystal Palace in 1903 and Prime Minister Balfour invited them to play before King Edward VII at Windsor, the journey to the castle being the occasion on which they were photographed here at Paddington. The card is anonymous and was posted in Manchester in September. 1905.

Paddington Station.   Tim and his Master.   Copyright.
Patronized by the King and Queen and other Members of the Royal Family.

BESSES-O'-TH'-BARN BAND.

BELOW: Built by the Great Western Railway and opened on 30th October 1871, Royal Oak was for many years the first stop out of Paddington for suburban trains. It is better known today as a station on the underground, on the Hammersmith & City line, which was a joint GWR and Met concern, having closed to main line trains in 1934. The station was eventually transferred to London Transport in 1970. Here we see the exterior of the typically GWR-looking building circa 1905, situated on Lord Hill's Bridge with a GWR covered dray in front. The bridge has today been rebuilt and the building seen here replaced, whilst the card is numbered 24674 but is anonymous.

TO THE ROYAL OAK STATION.

ROYAL OAK STATION. W. 24674.

After leaving Royal Oak, the Hammersmith & City trains needed to cross the main lines in order to turn away to the south at Westbourne Park. This was facilitated by the construction of a fly-under, which opened in 1878. Here, a westbound express crosses over the underground lines behind 'Badminton' Class 4-4-0 No. 3302 *Charles Mortimer*. New in July 1898, this engine was named just *Mortimer* until August 1904 and became No. 4110 under the 1912 renumbering scheme. The H&C line was electrified in 1905, giving us a time frame for the picture. In fact No. 3302 had a new boiler fitted in March 1911, which further restricts the date. Note the semaphore arms are all lettered – 'To CDS', 'To SL', 'To RL', 'To EL', etc – rather than having the usual white stripes, indicating which line the signal controlled. On the right, Subway Junction signal box is visible just above the exit from the fly under on this Locomotive Publishing Company card.

"The Queen" G.W. Railway.

Some superb locomotive portraits were taken at Westbourne Park shed over the years and this is one such example. Royal trains were always seen as something special but perhaps even more so than usual on this occasion, which was the journey of Queen Victoria from Windsor to London for her 1897 Jubilee celebrations. The express engine, standing in front of the shed, is another of the 'Achilles' Class 4-2-2s, No. 3041 *Emlyn*, which for this occasion had been renamed *The Queen*. It subsequently retained this until being renamed again in 1910, when it became *James Mason*. The Dean 'Singles', which many connoisseurs believe to be amongst the most elegant and beautiful locomotives ever built, certainly by the GWR, had desperately short careers, being superseded first by 4-4-0s and then 4-6-0s as express trains became heavier. No. 3041 was a prime example, being new in 1894 and withdrawn in November 1912; none of the class remained in service after 1915 and by the end, their brass boiler domes had been painted over, beading and crests removed, tender rails plated over and the splashers painted green instead of Indian red. It is understood that when the train ran with the Queen on board, the engine also carried the Royal Standard on the front buffer beam, possibly using the fixing seen by the brake pipe. The long since demolished Paddington Workhouse features in the left background, with the chimney and roof of the Atlas Iron Works in front.

RIGHT: Westbourne Park shed was situated very near to Paddington station, on a site that limited any expansion, hence it was replaced by a new depot at Old Oak Common opened in 1906. This overall view of Westbourne Park was probably taken shortly before it closed and certainly the roof on the left has lost some slates. In the foreground is 'Achilles' Class 4-2-2 No. 3012 *Great Western*, which was withdrawn in May 1909. Left of that is open cab 2-4-0T No. 3594, a 'Metropolitan' Class built in October 1899 that survived until May 1947. Cabs were generally fitted to the 'Metro' tanks in the 1920s but in earlier days the crews were expected to be tougher, even having to deal with the fumes when working on the underground lines; these little engines could also easily handle fast local passenger turns. There is another unidentified Dean 'Single' on the right and several 0-6-0 saddle tanks to be seen. The photograph was taken from Green Lane Bridge, with the bulk of the Paddington Workhouse again in the background, whilst the towpath of the Grand Union Canal ran behind the brick wall in the middle distance. Today, the A40 expressway now runs across the site of the depot. The card is one of three views of the shed produced by Pouteau about 1908.

G.W.R. NEWBURY RACE SPECIAL, FRENCH ENGINE No 103.

LEFT: Just beyond Green Lane Bridge, carrying Great Western Road over the line, was Westbourne Park station, where this anonymous card shows a Race Special heading for Newbury behind one of the French Atlantic engines, No. 103. The locomotive was built in mid 1905, in France at the Belfort Works of Société Alsacienne des Constructions Mechaniques, one of three that constituted Churchward's flirtation with Compound engines. No. 103 was to be named *President* in 1907 and later received many GWR fittings, which did away with its French looks but it appears to be in original condition here and yet to be named, whilst the chimney was fitted with a GWR style copper cap mid-1906, so the picture predates that. No. 103 was condemned in March 1927. The building in the left background is Westbourne School; the A40 expressway also now cuts through its site, to cross the line here.

RIGHT: This busy scene at Westbourne Park station is of particular interest as it seems to show *Emlyn* again but this time the name is on No. 3071, not No. 3041. Viscount Emlyn was Chairman of the GWR from 1895 to 1905, so of course an engine would bear his name. However, rather than rename No. 3041 again, the name was bestowed on a new 'Achilles' Class engine, No. 3071, built in February 1898. Coming from Paddington is another of the 'Achilles' Class, No. 3029 *White Horse*. Built in November 1891 as a 2-2-2, rebuilding to a 4-2-2 took place in July 1894. No. 3029 was withdrawn in May 1909, while No. 3071 survived until 1914, having had a new boiler in late 1910. Westbourne Park main line platforms closed on 16th March 1992 but the underground station is still open. The picture was published by Pouteau circa 1908.

Opening on 17th March 1906, the shed at Old Oak Common, built on the site of what had been open farmland, was a very necessary replacement for the overcrowded establishment at Westbourne Park. Here we see the interior of two of the four roundhouses, with everything looking quite new in this anonymously published view. Up to a hundred locomotives could be accommodated under cover, with two roundhouses for goods engines and two for passenger. In addition, there was a substantial works where quite extensive repairs could be undertaken. Identifiable here on the right – and helping us to date the picture – is No. 4003 *Lode Star*, which was new in to service in February 1907. On the left is 'Atbara' Class 4-4-0 No. 3391 *Wolseley*, built in September 1900 and fitted with a D3 type boiler in April 1907, so this view is post that date as well. At least one more 'Star' Class can be seen in the left centre background. Although superheated in July 1910, No. 3391's career lasted only until October 1928 but *Lode Star* fared better; fitted with superheating in May 1911, it was to be withdrawn by BR in July 1951. Old Oak Common has also become a memory, the last remaining GWR structures having been cleared by 2011, after the site was compulsorily purchased for use by the Crossrail project. A new depot is under construction on part of the site to service the trains for Crossrail, which is due to open throughout in December 2018.

A job that could not be avoided in the days of steam was the lighting of fires, for which oil-soaked rags and timber would be used, resulting in a great deal of filthy smoke. This odd looking device was an attempt to avoid the problem. The lower cylinder contains compressed air while above is an oil reservoir. The pipe leading into the cab enabled a fine spray of oil to be pumped into the firebox, where it could readily be ignited providing a flame over the dead coal. A detailed description may be found in *The Locomotive Magazine* for February 1913, pages 32-33, which was accompanied by this photograph. The device was patented by Mr J. Armstrong, shed master at Old Oak, and Mr W. Rogers, one of his assistants, but it is not known how successful it was nor how long it remained in use. The engine is 'City' class 4-4-0 No. 3439 *City of London*, which was new in May 1903 and which was to become No. 3716 in the GWR's December 1912 renumbering. It was withdrawn from service in April 1929. This is a 1930s printing of a Locomotive Publishing Co. card that would have probably first appeared in 1913.

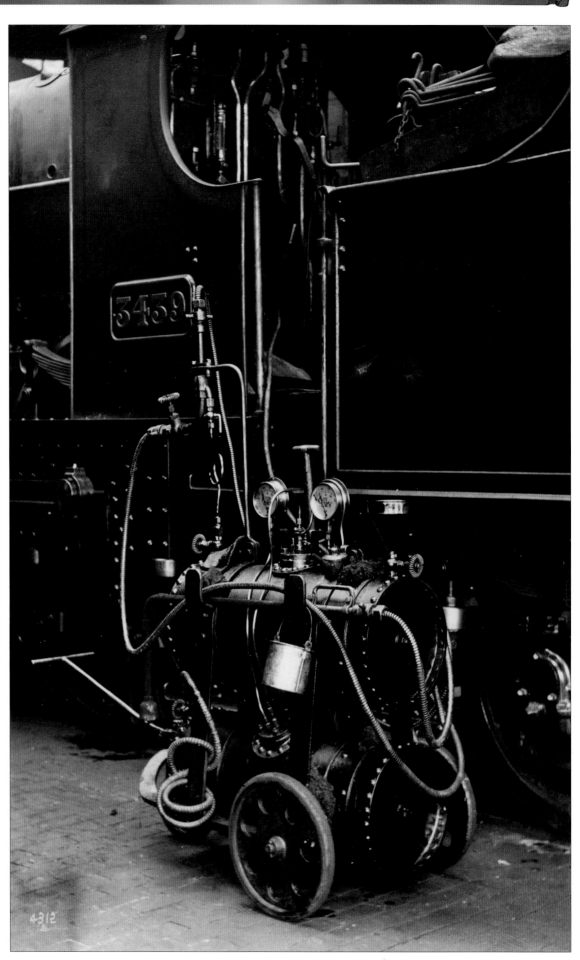

ABOVE: There are few GWR stations in the area being covered so here we are stretching things a little to the west, to take in a view of Acton station on another of the cards by Pouteau. A Down local stands at the platform where there are a few passengers to be seen. The engine is 'Duke' Class 4-4-0 No. 3323 *Mendip*, built in June 1899. Its name was originally on a straight plate but the later style of curved name had been fitted by the date of this picture. Its boiler was first replaced in January 1907 and the picture looks to predate that change. Unlike a number of the class, No. 3323 (which became No. 3277 in 1912) was not rebuilt as a 'Bulldog' and survived until March 1936. Note the unusual double loading gauge on the left, where there is a notice 'LOOK OUT FOR LOAD GAUGES'. Opened on 1st February 1868 as Acton, the station has been known as Acton Main Line since 1st February 1949 but little remains of that seen here; Platform 1 and all of the buildings have been demolished and Platform 2 is not used. There is a small modern building at road level with just an outside ticket counter and a small shelter is provided on each platform.

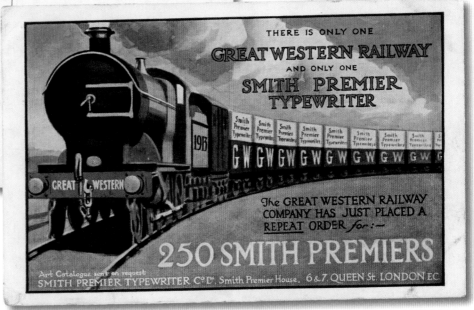

ABOVE AND RIGHT: This is an easy card to date, as the Smith Premier Typewriter Co. Ltd used the year – 1913 – as the locomotive number. The advertisement certainly also served to put the railway name into the public eye but were the GWR consulted? And would it have found favour in other areas where Smith's had but where other railway companies held sway?

Heading back in to central London, we also return to LB&SCR territory for this final GWR view. In 1910, Great Western trains operated in to Victoria station every hour or so. They ran from various stations on the GWR main line, some from as far out as Windsor and they worked round from the GWR via Kensington and Battersea. This is yet another Pouteau view, with the ex-LC&DR Grosvenor Road signal box on the right (the rear of the LB&SCR box can just be seen on the left), the picture being taken from Grosvenor Road station. The station had two sides, that to the east serving LC&DR trains having opened on 1st November 1867, whilst the LB&SCR opened their platforms immediately to the west three years later to the day; however, both had been used as ticket platforms for Victoria since January 1867. The LB&SCR shut their side on 1st April but the SE&CR platforms (as they now were) remained for a little longer, closing on 1st October 1911. The station straddled the north end of Victoria Bridge, which also spanned Grosvenor Road. A GWR 2-4-0T heads south towards Battersea with a train of mostly 6-wheelers. There is a horse box at the head of the train, which would be carrying the horse and driver for the dray on the carriage truck immediately behind. The rear of one of Peabody Avenue's terraces can be seen in the background and there were extensive carriage sidings between the houses and the train.

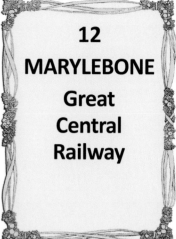

12 MARYLEBONE Great Central Railway

On 15th March 1899, Marylebone station opened, the last of the main line termini in London. No artist is credited for this picture of the concourse, which was published by Raphael Tuck in December 1906, in their 'London Railway Stations' Series II. Note just over the bookstall an advertisement for their postcards has been included. Over the years parts of this concourse have featured in films and television dramas, not least because the station could at times be very quiet. In fact, serious consideration was given to turning it into a bus station (1984) but fortunately this idea was dropped after two years of uncertainty. Today the station once again has main line trains, having lost such services in 1965 when the main line north of Aylesbury closed.

A smart looking GCR 4-4-0 stands at Marylebone station having just arrived on an express, whilst a gentleman wearing a bow tie strides purposefully towards the exit. The cab road is to the right and there are quite a number of milk churns in view. The engine is not positively identified but is probably Class '11B' No. 1038, which was also later to appear again on a coloured card. This one was published by Charles Martin and dates from about 1905.

No terminal station is complete without a bookstall and this panorama looking across the W.H. Smith kiosk gives a good general view of the platforms. Perhaps the train behind the bookstall is the one just seen on the previous page, for this is also a Charles Martin card and has the next number. Surprisingly for a station with a W.H. Smith bookstall, no Kingsway Series card of Marylebone has come to light. Much of the area under the canopy has been remodelled to cope with the increase in traffic and perhaps emphasising the folly that was almost committed with the proposed closure of the station, the cab road has now gone, to be replaced by tracks serving two additional platforms. Note the board on the right pointing to the Hotel Great Central adjoining the station – no self respecting railway company opened a major city terminus without building a hotel next to it – whilst on the left a similar board advertises the GCR's Royal Victoria Station Hotel in Sheffield. The GCR was named the Manchester, Sheffield & Lincolnshire Railway until 1897, the change in title coming about just before the opening of its London Extension line from Annesley in Nottinghamshire in 1899. It was originally intended to reach Marylebone by running over Metropolitan metals from Quainton Road but the two companies fell out and so agreement was reached instead with the GWR to come in via High Wycombe.

LEFT: This photographic view by John Walker & Co. gives a more detailed view of part of the concourse. Note the finger boards on the left ready to point at a departure at the time shown on the clock. The quiet scene is typical of the station over many years, as it always suffered from having to compete with the larger and far longer established termini of the other companies. The station is actually busier today than at any stage in its history. Note the two clerestory roofed GCR carriages just seen through the canopy in the centre left background. The card was posted in July 1906.

RIGHT: Waiting to depart from what was then Platform 4 is Robinson Class '11B' No. 1038 again but this time clearly identified. Built by Sharp, Stewart & Co. in March 1903, the engine received superheating equipment in October 1914. It was renumbered twice by the London & North Eastern Railway after Grouping, becoming No. 6038 in December 1925 and then No. 2322 in September 1946. It was withdrawn by British Railways in January 1949, probably without ever getting to wear its allotted BR number, which simply added a '6' prefix to its last L&NER number. The card is one of the F. Moore paintings from the Locomotive Publishing Co., published circa 1910.

LEFT: The goods station at Marylebone was considered to be the largest in London and clearly required many staff to look after things. There are ninety-six of them posing for this 14th November 1908 photograph, all men. These would be the office staff responsible to the Chief Goods Manager, who is thought to be the man sat slightly slouched seventh from the left in the front row. His name was C.T. Smith and he was to die whilst still in office on 10th May 1912. The bald headed, moustachio'd gentleman on his left is his assistant, E.A. Clear, who was appointed Assistant to the General Manager after Smith's death, succeeding Joseph Rostern who became the new Chief Goods Manager. No doubt other railways would argue as to which was actually the largest of the various goods depots but what is without question is that it was the GCR's London goods traffic which sustained the extended line for many years, rather than its generally lightly used passenger services.

The Great War brought many changes, one of which was the employment of women by the railways to take up the jobs that had been done by men who had gone to fight. This superb social history postcard, taken in Marylebone goods depot on 5th May 1917, shows that they were not just kept in the offices. Indeed, many found themselves undertaking quite heavy manual labour due to the depleted nature of the general workforce. By this date a picture of the clerical staff would show women as well, which may well include the lady on the right, equipped with pencil and notebook and engaged on goods checking duties. The men assisting with the unloading of the Great Eastern open wagon would have been too old or otherwise unfit for military service. It is undoubtedly the case that the wholesale mobilisation of the female workforce during the First World War, to undertake many of the heavy, dirty and onerous manual tasks previously done by men, as well as more skilled jobs such as working in offices and driving buses, did much to bring forward the legislation granting voting rights to women. It is arguable, in fact, that the contribution of women to the war effort achieved more than the suffragette movement managed with their often militant tactics in the decade leading up the 1914. The card was published by W.D. Marquis, about whom nothing is known. However, the card is No. 5, which suggests there are another four at least still to find! As an incidental point of interest, few postcards other than patriotic efforts or war scenes that had been approved by the official censor were published between 1914 and 1918, which not only makes this view doubly rare but is also worth remembering when attempting to date real photographic scenes on old cards.

RIGHT: Just outside Marylebone was a popular place for photographers, where a clear view could be obtained of trains just starting out on their journey. Here, a suburban train leaves for Aylesbury behind an unidentified Class '9N' 4-6-2T which would date from 1911, probably the year that the picture was taken. These engines were around for many years and at least one was still operating between Northwood and Aylesbury in the 1950s, with the last (reclassified as 'A5') going in 1960.

BELOW: One of the graceful Robinson 'Atlantics', Class '8B' No. 358, heads for the north with a Dining car express. Built in May 1906 and seen here probably just before the Great War, the engine just got into British Railways time, being withdrawn as No. 2920 in June 1948. From April 1925 to August 1946 it had been No. 5262.

LEFT: The London engine shed of the GCR was just at the edge of the area being explored, at Neasden. This is an early view with Pollitt designed 4-4-0 No. 269 posing for the picture. The engine is highly polished and decorated with flags on the smokebox door and the company crest on the bufferbeam, having worked one of the trains celebrating the opening of the London Extension in March 1899. Behind the engine is the coaling stage, from which No. 269 has just filled its tender, topped by a large water tank. There is a signal just to be seen on the left, which is on the West London line and is clear for a train heading towards Willesden. No. 269 very briefly became No. 269A when built in December 1897, the 'A' being dropped after just a couple of months. Renumbered by the L&NER as No. 5269 in August 1924, the engine was withdrawn in November 1932. The site of the shed has been totally redeveloped.

A useful connecting line runs north to south across west London from Willesden Junction to Clapham Junction. In pre-Grouping days, its ownership was complicated. At the north end, between Willesden and Kensington it was the West London Railway, opened on 27th May 1844 as a single line of mixed standard and broad gauge rails but which saw little use. The West London Extension Railway was then opened on 2nd March 1863, as the title suggests extending the line onwards from Kensington to Clapham Junction. This encouraged the L&NWR and GWR to take a joint lease of the WLR, whilst the WLER was a joint venture between those two companies, who took a third share each, with the final third being split equally between the L&SWR and LB&SCR. North and south of Kensington was thus under different ownership and both companies remained independent until Nationalisation in 1948. This L&NWR poster card of February 1910 advertised through services between Liverpool and Manchester – which joined at Crewe – to Brighton and Eastbourne on the south coast via the WLR/WLER. At Rugby, through carriages from Birmingham were also added to the train. Onwards travel from Willesden was behind LB&SCR locomotives and the trains, which were no doubt aimed at holidaymakers, included a Luncheon car.

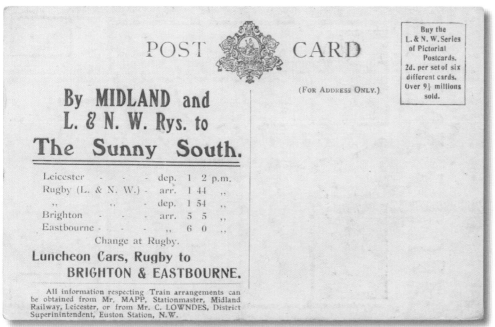

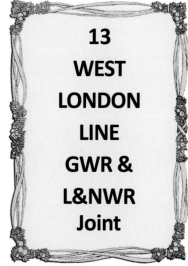

13
WEST
LONDON
LINE
GWR &
L&NWR
Joint

The reverse of the card opposite, which interestingly shows a connection that the poster itself does not, involving another railway company. Passengers could also travel from the Midland Railway's Leicester station and join the train at Rugby. Note the figure given for official cards sold by the L&NWR in the stamp space.

A busy scene outside Uxbridge Road station, where the West London Railway sign over the entrance held a long list of possible destinations. The most frequent services in 1910 were every half hour between Broad Street and Earls Court, and every 15 minutes between Addison Road and Aldgate. Along Uxbridge Road itself are horse buses plying between Shepherds Bush and Liverpool Street, mixing with delivery drays and carts. The station opened on 1st November 1869 and was closed on 21st October 1940, having been severely damaged by German bombs during September and October 1940. The street level building seen here remained until 1968, when it was demolished to allow for the construction of the Shepherd's Bush roundabout, in connection with the building of the M41 motorway (now redesignated as the A3220 dual carriageway). The last track level vestiges of the old station were obliterated when a new station was under construction in 2005, which finally opened on 28th September 2008. The card, by Charles Martin, was posted in December 1905.

A later and more full on view of Uxbridge Road station building, with the WLR sign over the entrance now fully readable, on a circa 1912 card by Johns. Indeed, the array of signage and notices around the station is bordering on the bewildering. Just beyond the station is the distinctive outline of The Royal Hotel, which was also lost in the late 1960s when the new motorway and roundabout were built. Several of those in the picture carry about their business oblivious to the photographer but the policeman and two gentlemen beneath Lockharts' blind and the uniformed railwayman partially hidden by the milk cart – what a gem! – are all aware of his presence. After the loss of its regular passenger service, the WLR/WLER line remained in use as a well-used freight artery, ensuring its survival. Today, the reinstated passenger services are operated by London Overground, with stations at Shepherds Bush (here at Uxbridge Road), Kensington Olympia, West Brompton and Imperial Wharf (a new site). Johns were prolific publishers of photographic cards of much of suburban London but little is otherwise known about the firm, such as where they operated from.

Just a little to the south is the station that was opened as Kensington on 2nd June 1862, becoming Kensington Addison Road in 1868. With the growing popularity of Olympia, which adjoined the station and was rather better known than Addison Road, the name was changed to Kensington Olympia at an unknown date. A spruce looking Beattie well tank, No. 190, built in December 1863, stands in the station with a train of close-coupled L&NWR 4-wheeled stock. L&NWR trains from Euston or Willesden to Waterloo, Cannon Street or London Bridge ran only between July 1865 and February 1868, and the rather official looking nature of the picture suggests a date possibly on or close to the inauguration of this service. At this time there were also regular GWR services on the line, resulting in the need for the mixed gauge track seen here, as the GWR was mainly broad gauge at that date. Indeed, it is thought that the train just visible in the north bay in the left background is broad gauge. Broad gauge passenger trains on the line ceased in 1866 but the GWR continued to run daily coal trains to Chelsea Basin for another decade at least. In August 1885, No. 190, seen here yet to be fitted with a rear weatherboard, was rebuilt as a 2-4-0 tender engine. The card, by the Locomotive Publishing Company, was issued in 1905.

This card is anonymous and was uncaptioned, although this was hardly required given the proximity of the station nameboard and the immediately recognisable nature of the building in the background. Behind the nameboard is the bay platform used by Underground trains from Earls Court. We can even accurately date the card, courtesy of the sign for Royal Naval & Military Tournament on the Olympia hall behind. This annual event began in 1880 and was held in the Royal Agricultural Hall until 1905, moving to Olympia for the first time in 1906. The 'MAY 21-JU 6' dates above the entrance mark this down as the 1908 tournament. The posters on display include one for Tuck postcards, second from the left.

We are so used to seeing Harry Beck's iconic 1933 map of the London Underground that it comes as something of a surprise to see it in this earlier geographical version, from a postcard published in 1908 and advertising the Great Eastern Railway's Liverpool Street Hotel on the reverse. Late the following year an updated version was produced, with a full advertising back, rather than the partial advertisement seen here, and with station names updated. The changes were to Gower Street, which became Euston Square in November 1909, and Euston Road which was changed to Warren Street in June 1908. The card was produced in English, French and German versions in connection with the Franco British Exhibition of 1908 and it also made early use of the 'UNDERGROUND' name, which had been agreed that year by the various railway companies, for use on stations and in advertising.

LIVERPOOL STREET HOTEL, E.C.,
adjoins the
LONDON TERMINUS OF THE
GREAT EASTERN RAILWAY
AND IS IN
DIRECT COMMUNICATION WITH
U LONDON UNDERGROUND D

SEE OVER.

POST CARD.

THE ADDRESS ONLY TO BE
WRITTEN ON THIS SIDE.

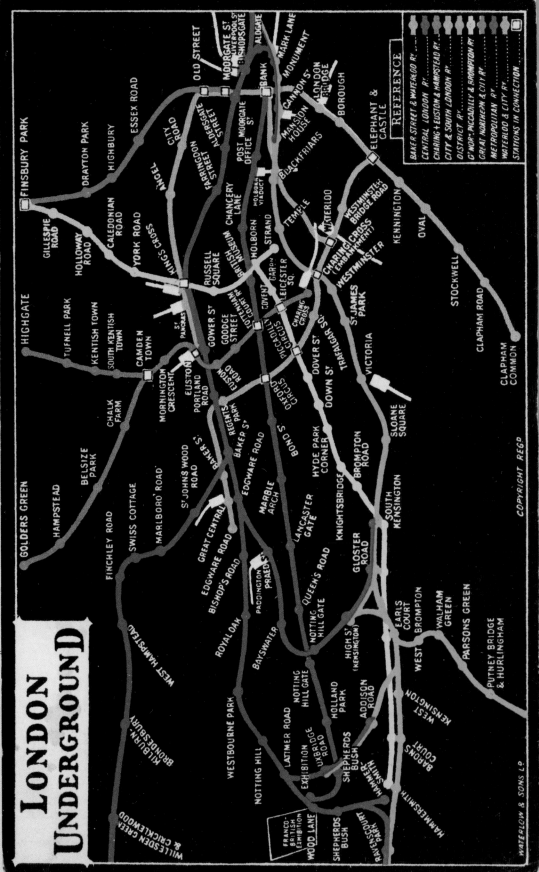

LONDON UNDERGROUND

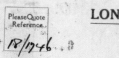

LONDON ELECTRIC RAILWAY.

PleaseQuote Reference

Oxford Circus (C.L) Str

Passenger Agent's Office, Electric Railway House, Broadway, Westminster, S.W.

Kitty Telfer

Dear Sir (or Madam),

I beg to remind you that your Season Ticket expires on *15 ⅸ 7 - 13.* and in anticipation of your desiring to renew it instructions are being given for a new three months' Ticket to be sent to *Finsbury Park* Station to await your call on the date of the expiry of your present Ticket, and if, therefore, any alteration in your Ticket be desired, I shall be glad if you will kindly **advise me by return of post.**

Should you however decide not to continue your present Ticket, I shall be obliged if you will kindly surrender it immediately on expiry.

Yours truly,

S. J. WEBB,

Passenger Agent.

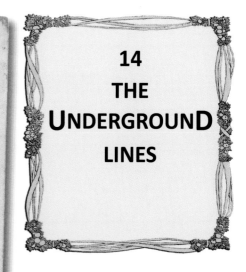

14
THE
UNDERGROUND
LINES

Hullo! Did you come by UNDERGROUND?

Photochrom Co., Ltd.

POST CARD

6.
7 JUL

HALFPENNY

J. H. Telfer Esq.
14, Clifton Rd:
Crouch End.
N.

LEFT AND ABOVE LEFT: Over the years there have been a great range of posters produced to advertise the UNDERGROUND. This delightful offering is by the well known children's artist Mabel Lucy Atwell, whose artwork featured heavily on postcards, as well as in books, on china, as figurines and a whole assortment of other items now considered as collectables. This poor condition but extremely rare postcard was used by the London Electric Railway in July 1913, to advise that a new three months' Ticket was being sent to Finsbury Park station to await collection by Kitty Telfer on the date of expiry of the current Season Ticket (note the use of capitals) and was printed 'Yours truly, S.J. WEBB, *Passenger Agent*'. UDG-030

41333. LONDON: KINGSWAY.
TRAVEL BY CENTRAL LONDON RAILWAY & ALIGHT AT MUSEUM STN

RIGHT: The Central London Railway made use of a set of six cards produced by the Photochrom Company, which were overprinted on the picture (on the back in another issue) with the name of the nearest station to the view depicted. The scenes were all ones to attract visitors and the cards were available by July 1911. The Gaiety Theatre on the right was built in 1903 but had become somewhat run down when it closed in 1939. It suffered bomb damage during the war and was demolished in 1956. CLR-001-1

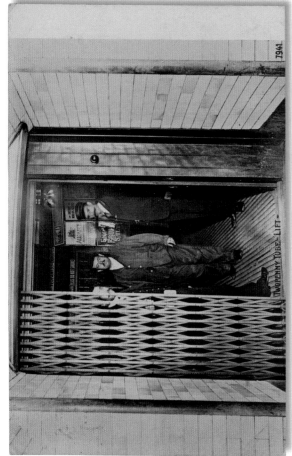

TWOPENNY TUBE · LIFT ·

TWOPENNY TUBE · LOCOMOTIVE ·

TWOPENNY TUBE · PLATFORM · BANK STATION ·

CLOCKWISE FROM TOP LEFT: A set of six cards of the CLR, known as the 'Twopenny Tube', were produced in Berlin and issued by Giesen Brothers of London E.C., starting with this view of the entrance to Post Office station in 1902, opened on 30th July 1900 and named after the nearby main Post Office. The architectural design could be recognised on all of the stations on the original line to Shepherds Bush. The shop by the entrance was typical, with one man here finding it warranted a good look. The name was changed to the more suitable St. Paul's, the cathedral being close by, in 1937, after the existing St. Paul's station on the old SER line was renamed Blackfriars (CLR-025). A view of one of the lifts, which were generally set up to have passengers in one side and out the other, helping to speed things up. The lifts were always operated by a liftman, although in later years this was more often a woman (CLR-026). A locomotive posed in an unidentified station. Trains on the Twopenny Tube were originally hauled by separate locomotives but it was not long before all the necessary equipment and motor were accommodated in the leading carriage. The 1938 stock was the first to be able to hide all this under the carriage. Note the wooden platform (CLR-028). The platform at Bank station. Although electrically lit, this shows well how the amount of light faded between lamps. It seems that there were posters on the wall probably from opening and whilst they have changed over the years, they have certainly served to brighten the stations up (CLR-030).

RIGHT: From Tuck's 'London Railway Stations' Series II 9383, the description on the reverse of the card is for the City & South London Railway. However, the caption 'Central Tube Station (London)' and the sign pointing to City & South London Railway suggests that Bank station on the Central London Railway is the probable location and the train looks right for the 'Twopenny Tube'. The set was issued in December 1906. Raphael Tuck established his business in London in 1866, moving from Germany with his wife Ernestine and seven children, some of whom later joined the firm. Consolidating in to grand new purpose built offices at Raphael House in 1899, on the corner of Moorfield and Temer Street, Raphael Tuck & Sons Ltd continued to grow and prosper despite the death of its founder in the following year. Sadly, the company's records were lost when Raphael House was destroyed by Germans bombs on the night of 29th December 1940.

CENTRAL TUBE STATION (LONDON)

5494   OXFORD CIRCUS & OXFORD STREET LOOKING EAST, LONDON.

LEFT: With a mix of motor and horse-drawn vehicles, Oxford Street looks as chaotic in this view from 1910 as it does nowadays. However, clearly the publishers felt it was not busy enough, as a little judicious early 20th century 'Photoshopping' has taken place; the bus seen rear on in the foreground, along with the motor car and bus coming towards it on the right, have all been cut out from other pictures and added to the original photograph. On the left is one of the Midland Railway offices that were to be found in many places, whilst on the right is the Bakerloo building with that of the CLR just across Argyll Street. The Bakerloo building has since had six more floors added on top but remains much the same at ground level. At the date of the picture the floors above the 'Twopenny Tube' station were used by the railway as offices and indeed it is from here that the Mabel Lucy Atwell card on page 151 was sent. The building today is little changed.

Tube Station, Notting Hill Gate.

LEFT: Built to an absolutely standard design, the Central London Railway station at Notting Hill Gate – seen here about 1905 – stood in an area that has in recent years seen much change and the old buildings have gone. The site, on the corner of Pembridge Gardens, is now occupied by a bank. The architect responsible for the CLR stations was Harry Bell Measures (1862-1940). During a long and varied career, Measures also designed high quality housing in London and the south east of England, later moving on to 'improved' workers housing in London and Birmingham and finally becoming Director of Barrack Construction for the British War Office during the First World War. He also designed the original Union Jack Club in Waterloo. Standing on the corner is a flower seller with a basket laden with blooms.

Holland Park Avenue.

Travelling one station further west we arrive at Holland Park. The station itself is on the north side of Holland Park Avenue, at the corner of Lansdowne Road. The standard style H.B. Measures building still remains and apart from traffic and road markings, the only obvious change today is that the trees have grown. The card, was published by Charles Martin about 1904.

Shepherds Bush, with its by now easily recognisable style of building, was originally the end of the line. The photographer was on Uxbridge Road, with Shepherds Bush Green behind and to his right. This was also the terminus for the trams but from the other direction and they were advertised as running in connection with the railway. Note the railings just visible on the right protecting a urinal. The station was completely rebuilt in 2007-08, in connection with the nearby development of the Westfield shopping area.

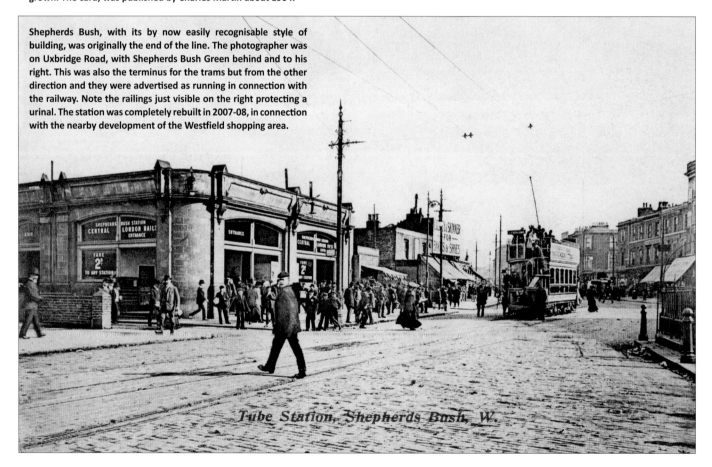

Tube Station, Shepherds Bush, W.

ABOVE: Pictures within pictures on this Central London Railway poster card. The map shows the extension to Wood Lane in place, which was opened in 1908. To the east, Bank was still the terminus but this would change in 1912, when the line was extended to Liverpool Street. Posters on the wall on the left advised of the benefits of using the CLR to reach theatres, halls and the shopping areas. CLR-013

ABOVE RIGHT: The CLR generated their own electricity at this power station built at White City, which was shown along with a route map on this card from about 1908. CLR-007

ABOVE AND LEFT: Two unusual pictures were taken at the CLR's power station site during the 1911 railway strike. Men who were still working stayed on site, presumably to avoid meeting with those out on strike, but with no proper accommodation available, they slept on roll up matteresses, some in what little shelter was afforded by the turntable pit and others alongside one of the buildings. The company produced these two cards as a thank you to those men, the second of which shows some of them relaxing but still with their hats on! The private owner wagon discernible in the picture above is labelled MYROS, which was the trade name for the coal factors Myers, Rose & Co. Ltd of London E.C. CLR-070/CLR-071

The Central London Line – A Comic Social History Interlude

This set of twelve cards of stations on the Central London Railway were the work of the well known Victorian cariacature and cartoon artist Phil May (1864-1903), who with his witty observations and economy of line, is now considered to be the father of modern cartoon illustration. They are presented here in order travelling west from Bank across central London to Shepherd's Bush. The second station, Post Office, was renamed St. Paul's in 1937, after the main line St. Paul's station became Blackfriars; Museum was actually named British Museum and closed in 1933 when the nearby Holborn station, on the Piccadilly Line, was enlarged to cater for Central Line trains as well and Queen's Road became Queensway in 1946. For some reason, Lancaster Gate was not included, the only station on the CLR to be omitted from the set, which was issued by Shurey's Publications, book and magazine publishers of Gough Square, London, circa 1903. The twelve cards are a lovely comic observation of late Victorian/ early Edwardian styles, from a hugely talented artist who suffered ill health for much of his life and died tragically early, aged just thirty-nine, of tubercolosis in 1903.

LONDON TUBE. CITY & SOUTH LONDON RAILWAY

LEFT: As on the CLR, early days on the City & South London Railway saw trains hauled by locomotives. The station shown here on this unusual but rather crude anonymously published half-tone card, used in August 1904, is not identified but there are still two on the line with the original island platform, at Clapham North and Clapham Common. Until the 1990s, Angel station had the same set-up, which at busy times could seem somewhat hazardous and it was rebuilt in the early 1990s to provide separate platforms, one being very wide as the old island was extended across the space previously taken by one of the lines.

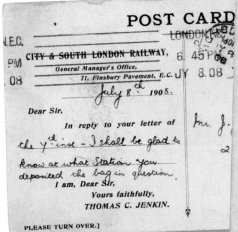

POST CARD

N.E.C.
PM
08

CITY & SOUTH LONDON RAILWAY,
General Manager's Office,
71, Finsbury Pavement, E.C.

July 8th 1908.

Dear Sir,
    In reply to your letter of the 7th inst – I shall be glad to know at what Station you deposited the bag in question.
    I am, Dear Sir,
        Yours faithfully,
        THOMAS C. JENKIN.

PLEASE TURN OVER.]

ABOVE AND RIGHT: Posted in July 1908, this unusual white on black map card was used by the City & South London Railway for correspondence from the General Manager's Office (Thomas C. Jenkin) at 71 Finsbury Pavement EC. Highlighted in the centre is the Euston to St. Pancras section of the C&SLR, which opened to traffic in 1907, the rest of the line having opened in 1900-1901. The lines of other railways, including numerous of the main line companies, also featured, showing how they dove-tailed with the burgeoning tube network, but prospective travellers were appraised of the benefits of under cover travel, 'without change of carriage', to and from stations both north and south of the river. CSL001.

Opened on 18th December 1890, Stockwell station was on the route of the C&SLR's line on its way to the terminus at Clapham Common. This extension had opened in December 1900, prior to which Stockwell had been the end of the line. Clapham Common then became the terminus for the next twenty-six years, until the extension to Morden opened in September 1926. The station, designed by T.P. Figgis and which had a fine domed roof over the two lifts that were provided, was closed from 29th November 1923 to 1st December 1924. The original island platform was replaced by a new station just to the south, with separate platforms and escalators replacing the lifts, as part of the modernisation work carried out in connection with the extension to Morden. The buildings seen here were replaced at that time and were replaced again when the station became an interchange with the Victoria Line. Posted in 1910, this view in the Card House Series contains much of period interest to study.

Just on the north side of the original Stockwell station was a siding leading up a steep slope to the east, where the C&SLR established a generating station, works and car sheds. This Locomotive Publishing Co. card shows locomotive No. 36, together with one of the cars in original condition. When built they were provided with high-backed seats for passenger comfort, which meant virtually no windows. This was not popular, however, as passengers wanted windows even if travelling underground, so the carriages were modified and passengers were happier. Power generation here ceased in 1915, and having provided a useful workbase and access point during the upgrading works, the site closed completely when these finished. It soon vanished beneath a large U-shaped block of flats, known as Stockwell Gardens.

GREAT NORTHERN & CITY TUBE

GREAT NORTHERN AND CITY TUBE. STEEL MOTOR COACH.

FINSBURY PARK TO MOORGATE IN 13 MINUTES.

THE ONLY QUICK ROUTE
BETWEEN
NORTH & SOUTH LONDON.

NO WAITING!! TRAINS EVERY 2 OR 3 MINS.

	FIRST TRAIN a m	LAST TRAIN p m
MOORGATE TO FINSBURY PK	5·55	11·20
Sundays	11·30	11·15
FINSBURY PK TO MOORGATE	5·40	11·10
Sundays	11·15	11·5

THROUGH BOOKINGS WITH:
GREAT NORTHERN RLY, METROPOLITAN, CITY & SOUTH LONDON RLY, AND LONDON BRIGHTON & SOUTH COAST RLY.

COMFORTABLE AND SPEEDY.   NO STRAPHANGING GOOD VENTILATION.

STATIONS

FINSBURY PARK, for Seven Sisters Rd Stroud Green Rd GREAT NORTHERN RLY. (stairs & lift Connection) Trams to Wood Green & Tottenham.

DRAYTON PARK, for Highbury Hill and Holloway.

HIGHBURY for Upper St, Highbury Fields and North London Ry Trams to Agricultural Hall, Angel and Highgate.

ESSEX ROAD, for New North Rd., Canonbury, Agricultural Hall

OLD STREET, for City Rd., Aldersgate St., Shoreditch, Goswell Rd., Hoxton; Trams to Commercial Rd and Poplar.

MOORGATE for Bank, The Metropolitan Ry, The City & South London Tube (for the Central London Tube and the Brighton & South Coast Ry)

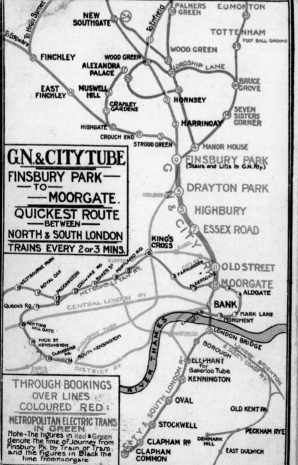

G.N. & CITY TUBE FINSBURY PARK — TO — MOORGATE. QUICKEST ROUTE BETWEEN NORTH & SOUTH LONDON TRAINS EVERY 2 or 3 MINS.

THROUGH BOOKINGS OVER LINES COLOURED RED: METROPOLITAN ELECTRIC TRAMS IN GREEN Note—The figures in Red & Green denote the time of journey from Finsbury Pk by Train or Tram and the Figures in Black the time from Moorgate

TOP: To advertise the line between Moorgate and Finsbury Park, the Great Northern & City Tube produced a set of postcards, probably in about 1905 although the earliest use so far recorded is from November 1907. It was unique amongst the London deep level lines, as it was constructed on a larger scale to allow main line trains to use it. The original trains were similar to the electric stock on the District Railway, which also was not a 'tube'. Otherwise, the card says it all. GNC-005

LEFT: This map card is from the same set and is the one coloured card that featured in it. Again it imparted plenty of information. GNC-006.

BELOW: One of the intermediate stations on the Great Northern & City, Essex Road opened on 14th February 1904. Published by J. Folkes of Islington, this view of it was probably taken soon after opening and whilst the card dates from that period, it was not posted until 1920. Note on the right there is again a board for Tidey & Sons which, as mentioned earlier, was the firm where H. Gordon Tidey worked. The building, less than beautiful perhaps but quite striking, remarkably still survives.

ELECTRIC RAILWAY STATION, ESSEX ROAD.

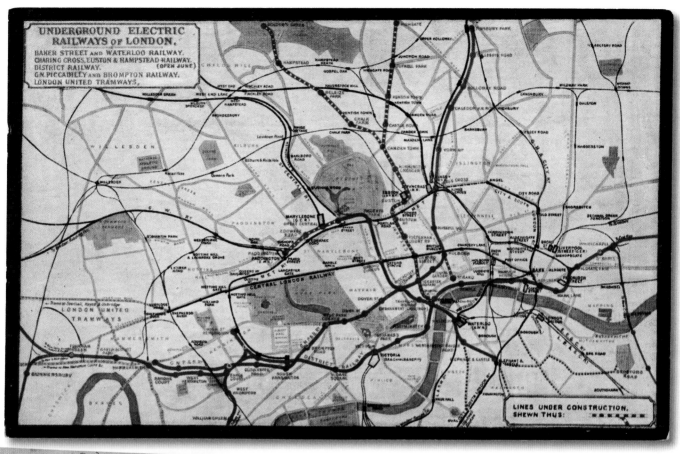

ABOVE: Opening on 15th December 1906, the Great Northern, Piccadilly & Brompton Railway issued two sets of cards, in December 1906 and February 1907, which were published for them by LPC and used F. Moore pictures. The map card, from the second set, shows the line from Finsbury Park making its way through Central London to Hammersmith. Useful to slip into a pocket, this might be why the card is the hardest of the set to find. GNPB-007.

LEFT: The power house at Lots Road in Chelsea will be a familiar sight to many. Published by Hartmann in about 1904, this card shows two gentlemen with a head for heights, no doubt part of the construction team, and it may well have been produced for the construction company, giving them some good publicity. The view of the power station is across the now redeveloped goods yard by Chelsea Basin, which was accessed from the West London line.

BELOW: Lots Road provided power for the Underground from 1905 to 2002, when the equipment reached the end of its life but the four chimneys had already been reduced to two when the station was converted to oil in the 1960s. Still with its two chimneys, it has now been incorporated into the Chelsea waterfront development. GNPB-009

ABOVE: A posed view of a train in the platform at Piccadilly Circus from the LPC in 1905. The lack of people and posters suggest that the picture was taken while testing was still being undertaken prior to opening and note the driver, with just a porthole to look through.

RIGHT: The Kingsway Series by W.H. Smith includes this view of Dover Street showing the exterior of the station. Opened with the GNP&BR on 15th December 1906, it was situated on the east side of the street, close to the Piccadilly end, and was easily recognisable, being in the usual house style. Dover Street station was rebuilt in 1933 with a new booking hall and entrance closer to Green Park, the name changing to Green Park at the same time. The old station entrance has now vanished and the site is occupied by No's 5 to 7 Dover Street, a modern brick building.

S.8455   DOVER STREET, PICCADILLY, LONDON.

South Kensington Tube Station, S.W.

LEFT: This view of the GNP&BR entrance to South Kensington station (correctly described on the card as a 'Tube Station') was taken when it was so new that the signs are still the temporary ones. In the entrance just right of the nearer boater-wearing gent can be seen a sign pointing to the Metropolitan and District booking offices, at the earlier sub-surface station serving those lines. Today the pale band across the terra cotta tiled frontage carries the station's name and the small black squares just discernible here show where preparations for attaching the letters had been made.

RIGHT: Posted in September 1907, this card shows the freshly opened Hampstead station on the Charing Cross, Euston & Hampstead Railway's tube line. The opening took place on 22nd June 1907 and the exterior has remained little changed over the years, although it seems a pity that the lettering has gone. The traffic is limited to one lady cyclist, who is just passing a policeman keeping a watchful eye on the photographer.

BELOW: Probably published in 1907, this postcard advertising the CCE&HR line carried an artistic view of Hampstead Heath, one of the capital's attractions that was now so much easier to reach. The painting, a pastiche of the classic English romantic style as pioneered and mastered by John Constable, carries a signature but is rather indistinct due to the size it was reproduced and the quality of the postcard's printing but possibly Wilson was the artist's name.

BELOW: Situated on Baker Street – made famous of course as the home of the fictitious detective Sherlock Holmes – the original Baker Street station, on the Baker Street & Waterloo Railway, soon to become known as the Bakerloo Line, was opened on 10th March 1906. Although this anonymous card, No. 21987, was not posted until September 1908, the picture was clearly taken close to the opening date. Note the man with the sandwich board, although unfortunately his movement meant the camera could not 'freeze' him and the message is thus unreadable. At this time, the platforms were only accessible by lifts, the first escalator coming into use in 1914. Subsequent developments mean that the original building seen here has vanished.

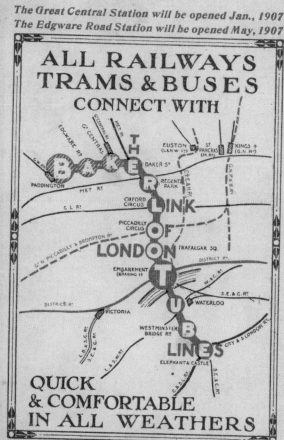

ABOVE AND RIGHT: Still with the Baker Street & Waterloo Railway, this map poster card was most likley issued in autumn 1906, at an important period in the rapid development of London's Underground network. The opening dates at the top refer to the extension of the line, already being referred to as the Bakerloo Tube, to Paddington, with new intermediate stations at Great Central (renamed Marylebone in 1917) and Edgeware Road; in the event they opened on 27th March and 15th June 1907 respectively. At the bottom, the opening dates of two further lines, the Great Northern, Piccadilly & Brompton Railway (which we have yet to visit) and the CCE&HR (previous page) are also noted. UDG-026.

BELOW: The Metropolitan Railway station at Farringdon, with a six car train of 1905 stock standing at the eastbound platform. Renamed Farringdon & High Holborn in 1922, the name was shortened again to just Farringdon in 1936. Today, the station is unrecognisable from this view, for it has been extensively rebuilt as part of the Crossrail development.

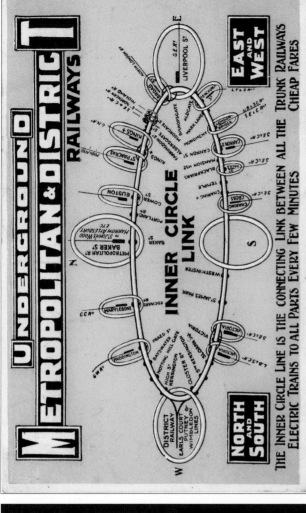

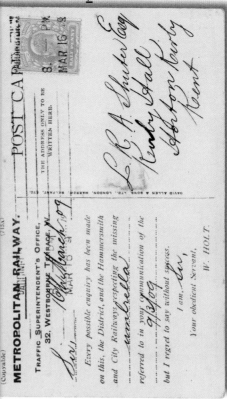

ABOVE AND RIGHT: The Metropolitan Railway used this sunshine yellow map poster card for correspondence in March 1909. was a reply from the Traffic Superintendent's Office with regard to a lost umbrella; every possible enquiry had been made but without success. MET-037

LEFT: Early days on the Metropolitan are depicted here on a card providing two views for the price of one and showing a Hammersmith train (TOP) and an Inner Circle train (BOTTOM), both at Aldgate. On the left of the lower picture another engine stands by the signal box, with a New Cross destination showing and on a short siding from which it could back straight onto a train in the terminating platform. There is no sign yet of any electrification work, so the views will be pre-1902. No. 55 was sold to R. Fraser in 1906 and may have been scrapped by them at Neasden, whilst No. 49 survived until 1936, being photographed at Neasden shed in 1934; both belonged to the 'B' Class. As can be imagined, underground steam hauled trains led to dirty, smoke-filled carriages and stations, and the opening of the electric CLR 'Twopenny Tube' line saw the Metropolitan and District railways haemorraging passengers in 1899-1900, forcing both in to electrification of their respective lines.

RIGHT: From their 'London Railway Stations' Series II (9383), this view outside Moorgate station also includes the Tuck offices at Raphael House beyond, with their flag flying ovehead, in an era when pedestrians could stroll in the street here. As noted earlier, the area suffered significant damage in the Blitz and more recently has undergone extensive redevelopment. As a result this view looking north in Moorfields is completely changed today. RT-704

BELOW: Portland Road station was at the time of this picture on an island surrounded by roads. The view is looking north to Holy Trinity church, on the far side of Euston Road. In 1917, the station changed its name to Great Portland Street and it was rebuilt on the same site in 1930, a building designed by C.W. Clark, which remains in use today and is now Grade II listed. This is a very different offering from Raphael Tuck, sent in May 1920.

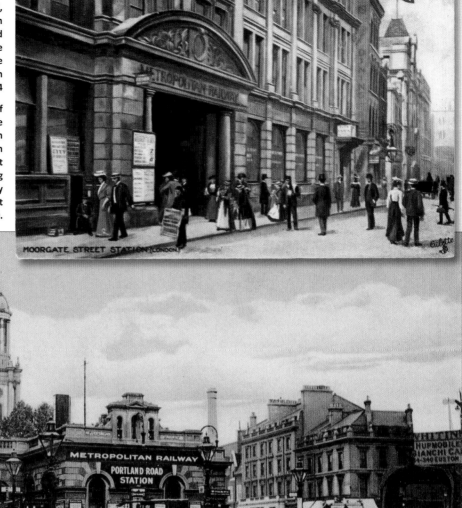

Portland Road Station.

LEFT: Heading further west we come to Paddington, where the Circle Line station was known for many years as Praed Street. Just before reaching the station, the line to Hammersmith branches off at Praed Street Junction and this is the interior of the signal box that controlled it. There is a board behind the levers stating what each one operates, whilst above is a shelf holding the telegraph instruments, which were used for communication and to show which parts of the line were occupied. Note the 'ghosts' of the signalman on the right and also of the levers that he had had to move during the long exposure required to take the picture. This is a Pouteau card from about 1906.

The station at Edgware Road was built in a shallow cutting, giving passengers a brief burst of daylight and fresh air. This view is looking east, with a steam-hauled Hammersmith train approaching and passing an electric unit heading away. Despite the very restricted nature of the site, its open to the air location led the Met to establish engine sheds, a carriage shop and a workshop here. On the right is part of the main engine shed, with the rear of an engine just peeping out. There was a second engine shed building on the left, behind the photographer, which was served by the two lines on the far left. The carriage shop was in the far right corner, behind the engine shed, and a traverser was installed in front of it, the only means by which carriages could be moved inside on this very restricted site; it could just about accommodate two carriages on each of its six roads. However, the end of steam and the introduction of electric multiple units saw the closure of all these facilities. Note that the expanse of wall on the left was not allowed to go to waste if advertising space could be sold. The card was issued by the Locomotive Publishing Company in 1905.

Between Baker Street and Finchley Road were three stations on the Metropolitan line that were all closed following the opening of the Bakerloo line extension in 1939. First of these was St. John's Wood Road, which had opened on 13th April 1868 and was closed on 20th November 1939. It is only partly visible on this card by Charles Martin about 1904, hidden by a horse bus showing the popularity of the upper deck. Also of interest are what appear to be two delivery tricycles on the left. The station was on the corner of St. John's Wood Road, close to Lords cricket ground. There was no direct replacement for it and all the buildings seen here have gone.

ST. JOHN'S WOOD ROAD STATION.

Marlborough Road Station & Queens Road, St. John's Wood, N.W.

ABOVE: The next call was at Marlborough Road, also opened on 13th April 1868. Closing on 20th November 1939, it was replaced by the nearby St. John's Wood station. Just for a change, the small shop in the station was not a tobacconist but a dyers and cleaners, whilst the end wall of the building next door was too good to be left blank, with three firms making use of it to display their businesses. Again by Charles Martin, the card was posted in December 1907.

BELOW: The third station, Swiss Cottage, opened and closed on the same dates, with the new station being given the same name. Another Charles Martin card, dating from 1904, note the greengrocer's display on the left, while the shop in the station is Fitzjohn's estate agents. On the wall above, the advertisement is for Houghton & Co., cheesemongers, poulterers and porkmen. All three of these stations were to the same design.

Finchley Road Station.

Situated on the corner of Finchley Road and Canfield Gardens, the station at Finchley Road was built in a different style. Opened on 30th June 1879, it was known by the name seen on the front of the building here, Finchley Road South Hampstead, from 1885 to 1914, when it reverted to plain Finchley Road. The view is looking north up Finchley Road towards the Midland station, which was on the left just past the row of buildings; interestingly, the large scale OS shows a physical connection between the MR and Met stations, via the goods yard of the former. Just beyond the MR station was the L&NWR's Finchley Road & Frognal station on their Hampstead Junction line. The Met line made its way south east from here beneath the photographer's feet and running parallel to it just to the west were the twin lines of the Great Central Railway heading to Marylebone. There is a neat 3-wheeled cart for milk deliveries in the right foreground and note the man in top hat and tails walking past. By Charles Martin again, the card was posted February in 1906.

We end this sequence of Charles Martin cards with this 1904 view of West Hampstead station. It was to a different design again, being built over the railway and facing West End Lane as it crossed the line. The corner of the station is again occupied by an estate agents. The straight backed lady on the left is passing two young boys wearing the sailor-type clothes popular at the time. The cyclists are all ladies, whilst heading the other way there is some work ahead for the coalmen on the well laden coal van.

WEST HAMPSTEAD. — WEST END LANE.

Willesden Green Station N.W.

Willesden Green & Cricklewood Station. MET.

ABOVE: There is a very good series of postcards featuring scenes around north west London and Middlesex with this very distinctive style of caption but they are anonymous – a shame as the photographer deserves recognition. Just look at the detail on this view of the road frontage of Willesden Green station; the posters merit careful study and there is an advertisement for Met Post Cards on the board between the two men on the right. Note, too, the 'UNDERGROUND' logo on a background of a silhouette of the London skyline above the posters. Opened by the Met on 24th November 1879, the station was known as Willesden Green and Cricklewood from 1st June 1898 until 1938. There is no indication of the longer name on this card, which was posted in August 1913, with just Willesden Green on the board above the entrance. The station is still in use today but this scene vanished in 1925, when the building was rebuilt to the design of C.W. Clark.

ABOVE AND RIGHT: Here on these two views, however, on cards from the same anonymous series as the exterior view – one of which was posted in September 1913 – we see the full name of Willesden Green and Cricklewood on the station nameboard. The bookstall belonged to W.H. Smith & Sons and beyond is one of the Finlay tobacco kiosks that were to be found on so many stations. Unlike the building at street level, the platform accommodation was not rebuilt in 1925 and consequently it remains much the same as seen here. Since 1940, the station has been served by tube rather than Met trains. The second picture was taken on the same occasion, probably a few minutes after the previous view, with the platform now devoid of passengers. The station master has barely moved but the bookstall manager has now come out to pose too. Note that the station name also featured on the backs of the platform benches.

Willesden Green & Cricklewood Station. MET.

RIGHT: Posted in August 1910, this card by Reeves shows the new station at Dollis Hill, which was opened on 1st October 1909. The name on the board shows Dollis Hill for Gladstone Park and this was briefly reflected in a change of name to Dollis Hill & Gladstone Park, which lasted only from 1931 to 1933. Looking at the lady holding on to her hat, it seems likely it was a breezy day! The view is looking north-west and the two non-electrified lines in the foreground are those of the Great Central Railway heading to and from Marylebone. The island platform was served by subway entrances on either side of the line and the buildings were replaced in the 1930s.

ABOVE: What chance today of seeing a gentleman on a horse in middle of the road outside Neasden station? It opened on 2nd August 1880 as Kingsbury & Neasden, which is the name displayed here. On 1st January 1910, the name was reversed to Neasden & Kingsbury and on 1st January 1932 it became plain Neasden, as it is still known today. It became a tube station following the opening of the Bakerloo Line to Stanmore in 1939, Met trains ceasing to call the following year. The buildings either side remain but the central house-like building has been replaced. The view, in the Kingsway Series, is looking north on Neasden Lane circa 1908.

LEFT: Some sources say Neasden was built with three platforms, yet there is no sign of a third platform here, nor on a large scale map of 1895 which shows just the two. When the line was quadrupled early in the Great War, many of the stations had to be rebuilt but not here as the additional lines were put through where the house is on the left, with the result that the platform buildings remain today. The view is looking back towards Dollis Hill and in the background, through the arch beneath the station building, can be seen the bridge carrying the Midland Railway's line between Dudding Hill and Harlesden. The card, by Reeves again, was posted in April 1911.

"Women's Work in Wartime".
Met. Ry. Assist. Guards.
"Consulting the Working
book."

"Women's Work in Wartime".
Met. Ry. Train Conductors.
"Awaiting their trains."

Opposite Page Top:
Metropolitan ladies pose for an anonymous photographer during the Great War, probably circa 1917. The location is Neasden station Down platform but the picture is not sharp enough to read either cap badges or words on collars, which could have given an idea as to what position the ladies were employed in. Nor is there any clue as to the role of the lady not in uniform. Neasden depot lay on the right of the line just beyond the bridge and the locomotive on the right had either been shunting the small yard here at the station or was waiting to access the depot.

Opposite Page Bottom and This Page Right:
These three superb privately produced studies form part of a correspondence between a Mr A.L.P. Reavil of Cleveland Square W2, who was writing to a Mr R.G. Armstrong of West Acton, who it seems worked for the GWR at Paddington. The handwriting on the rear matches the inscriptions on the front, so it may well be that Reavil himself took the photographs, which he entitled '*Women's Work in Wartime*'. The picture of '*Met. Ry Assist. Guards Consulting the Working Book!*' was taken at Neasden but there is no location for the '*Conductors. Awaiting their trains*', although the station should be recognisable to some; '*A Smart Train Conductor. Hammersmith & City Line*' was also at Neasden. All were probably taken in 1917 but they were sent in August 1917, January 1918 and February 1919 respectively. These may well be true 'one-off' cards.

Women's Work in Wartime.
A Smart Train Conductor.
Hammersmith & City Line.

RIGHT: Published by Serjeant of Ladbroke Grove about 1904, this delightfully peaceful scene is looking north past Ladbroke Grove station. Opened as Notting Hill on 13th June 1864, '& Ladbroke Grove' was added in 1869 but in 1919, the name was changed again to Ladbroke Grove (North Kensington) and it then became plain Ladbroke Grove in 1938. In this view, the walls under the bridge and on adjacent buildings are as usual all covered with advertising. Viewed from the same point today, the scene can be recognised from the ends of the platform canopies which remain, although there is a more modern entrance, whilst the A40 Expressway now crosses over Ladbroke Grove right behind the railway bridge.

LADBROKE GROVE & STATION.

Hammersmith Station.

LEFT: In the Edwardian period it must have been easy to suffer from advertising overload for yet again we see posters plastered prolifically over almost every available surface. The scene is at Hammersmith and shows the second Met station which opened on 1st December 1868, when the line was extended a short distance. The building has all but vanished under the weight of advertising. The card is anonymous but was actually published by Blum & Degen, whilst although it was posted in August 1907, the picture was probably taken two or three years earlier.

60460. HAMMERSMITH STATION.

LEFT: Posted in April 1909, this Bell Series card, shows the station building as greatly improved not long before that date, with the joint GWR and Met ownership clearly displayed along the canopy and on the façade below the clock. The canopy has since been removed but the distinctively shaped frontage remains, facing on to Beadon Road. The building to the right, here still plastered with advertisements albeit a different selection from the earlier view, has also not survived. The original card is badly faded and was produced from what was clearly a rather distressed glass plate but views of the newly rebuilt station are rare.

LEFT: Covered in lettering and posters, just about the only thing missing from this view of the rather unprepossessing Charing Cross District Railway station is its name. The 'New Direct Through Route' referred to had been opened in 1902, with this picture probably taken just a year or so later. Part of the old roof of Charing Cross station can be seen in the left background, prior to its collapse in December 1905. The station was opened as Charing Cross by the District Railway on 30th May 1870. It was not until 1974 that the name was changed to Charing Cross (Embankment) and two years later it became plain Embankment. The entrance to the station was rebuilt when the CCE&HR arrived in 1914, giving the attractive frontage seen today.

RIGHT: A circa 1904 study of Victoria Street by Charles Martin, looking towards Parliament Square. The street has been completely changed by redevelopment, with only the tower of Westminster RC cathedral still surviving from this view today. All of the buses plying their trade and the cabs lined up in the middle of the road waiting for custom are horse-drawn. The District Railway's Victoria station just gets into the view on the right and next door is a Midland Railway office.

BELOW: A postman crosses the street on this Charles Martin view of Sloane Square station, situated at the south-east corner of the Square and opened on 24th December 1868. Having been rebuilt in the late 1930s, the station subsequently suffered serious damage during the Second World War but was rebuilt afterwards in the same style. More recently, an office block has been constructed above it. The array of posters again merit careful study.

Victoria St. S. W.

Sloane Square Station, Chelsea. S. W.

WEST KENSINGTON STATION

D & CO

The conveniently situated The Three Kings Hotel remains next to West Kensington station today, although it now trades as the Famous 3 Kings. It has been modernised at ground floor level but the advertising panel remains, albeit it is now plain white. The station, which faces west on North End Road close to the junction with Talgarth Road, was rebuilt in the late 1920s to the design of Charles Holden and is the building still in use today. This is the original District Railway station which opened on 9th September 1874 as North End (Fulham), becoming West Kensington on 1st March 1877. In this picture from about 1912, the District Railway name has been demoted to the side panels and 'UNDERGROUND' is now emblazoned over the entrance, with each letter in a separate panel. The Midland Railway goods office just creeping in to view on the right stood above the company's twin tracks leading to their Earl's Court coal depot. This was established in 1878, after the Midland had acquired an interest in the District Railway's Richmond extension three years earlier, allowing their coal trains in to the heart of west London. The policeman watching the D & Co photographer is standing in front of the offices of Spenser Whatley Ltd, coal merchants. Note the right-hand Midland poster is the one that features on the official postcard shown on page 24.

BARONS   COURT   STATION   D & CO

The now Grade II listed building at Barons Court is certainly worth a visit today, remaining virtually as seen here in this view taken in the years just after opening. This had occurred on 9th October 1905, the station being provided to meet the growing demand in the area and it was shortly afterwards to be served as well by the Hammersmith extension of the GNP&BR, whose underground rails reached the surface just to the west. The picture may in fact be from 1908 or soon after as, according to Transport for London, the distinctive 'UNDERGROUND' logo was first used in that year.

The 'other' Hammersmith station, opened on 9th September 1874, was for a few years the terminus of the District Railway following its extension from Earl's Court. It became a through station in 1877, when the line was extended again to join up with the L&SWR at Ravenscourt Park, with services then being extended over

L&SWR metals to Richmond. A year later, the Midland also began running through with their short-lived St. Pancras to Earl's Court via Dudding Hill service, whilst as illustrated on one of the introductory pages to this book, in 1894 the GWR began running through as well with their Ladbroke Grove to Richmond local trains. In 1906, the GNP&BR arrived and a new station was designed for that event by H.W. Ford. Posted in April 1908, this busy scene was probably photographed soon after completion, as there are still 'To Let' signs displayed, no 'UNDERGROUND' logo features as yet and the traffic is all horse-drawn, apart perhaps from the bus partly in view on the right. The 'uniform' standing four-square and watching the photographer may be an an omnibus inspector. The station and Hammersmith Broadway as seen here were all lost to redevelopment in the early 1990s and the entrance is now almost hidden in a shopping centre. Note the rather grand sounding dentists – Robinson's American Teeth Institute – above A.L. Jones & Co. Ltd's tobacconists shop on the right.

RIGHT: Looking north on Turnham Green Terrace, the station has its name clearly painted on the bridge, a common practice at the time as we have seen, although it was just out of sight on the right. On the left is the original signal box for Turnham Green Junction, where the District and L&SWR lines split. The card is from the Wyndham Series, circa 1904 and many of the buildings can still be seen today.

BELOW: The L&SWR opened the station at Turnham Green on 1st January 1874. This view from Back Common, at the eastern end of Acton Green, gives a very rural feel; published by E.C. Morgan & Co., it was posted in July 1905, when the line was still double track. The L&SWR quadrupled the line from Studland Street Junction (just east of Ravenscourt Park station) in 1911 and the new signal box seen here had to be rebuilt again, on the south side of the line. L&SWR services ceased in 1916, after which the route reverted to just two lines, only becoming four again when the Piccadilly tube was extended from Hammersmith to Hounslow in 1932.

BELOW: Whilst the L&SWR and District lines separated at Turnham Green station, it was a little further on at Chiswick Park that they turned away from each other, towards Richmond and Acton respectively. Chiswick Park was a District station and was opened as Acton Green on 1st July 1879. Renaming to Chiswick Park & Acton Green occurred in March 1887, with the change to plain Chiswick Park being completed on 1st March 1910. The entrance is at the junction of Bollo Lane (left) and Acton Lane and on this view, posted in August 1913, both District Railway and 'UNDERGROUND' are displayed. The poster on the gate pillar far left advertises the Army Pageant held in the summer of 1910 at Fulham Palace, which gives a more accurate date for the picture. The station was to be rebuilt to one of Charles Holden's circular designs, which was completed and opened in 1932.

Walham Green Station & Town Hall, Fulham.

LEFT: Walham Green station opened on 1st March 1880 and this Charles Martin card, which dates from 1903 or 1904 and shows an early motor bus waiting outside, has captured the original building, situated opposite Fulham Town Hall. The card was used in September 1906 although by that date the station had been rebuilt. The Town Hall still remains, however.

RIGHT: Walham Green station was rebuilt in 1905 to the design of H.W. Ford, in order to be able to handle the crowds at the newly opened Stamford Bridge football stadium of Chelsea FC. The building was closed as a station in 2003, when it was replaced by a shiny new facility inside a shopping precinct built next door; however, it still survives, now Grade II listed although currently out of use. 'UNDERGROUND' on the canopy suggests a date of 1908 or later for the picture. The Walham Green name remained in use until 1952, when the Fulham Chamber of Commerce succeeded in their campaign and it became Fulham Broadway. The card was published by Temperton's Stationery Stores in Fulham.

Broadway, Walham Green. S.W.

548 B. Walham Green Station.

LEFT: This rustic south-west looking view at Walham Green is no more, the platform now being surrounded by development and also having an overall roof. Although not posted until 1921, this early and rather crudely tinted card, published by Gordon Smith of Stroud Green Road, Finsbury Park, would date to about 1904. The buildings feintly visibly in the right background were a smithy, which had closed shortly before the picture was taken. The nearer building seen side on was then enlarged and converted to show early movies, being marked as a 'Picture Theatre' on a large scale 1906 OS and then as a 'Cinema' on a 1916 edition.

LEFT: Posted in 1908, this card shows a steam hauled District Railway train bound for Wimbledon paused at East Putney station. Electric trains started running here on 27th August 1905, so the picture clearly pre-dates that and is probably late 1890s. Opened on 3rd June 1889, this is the first L&SWR station on this route that we visit, their platforms being those on the right here. The L&SWR built the line from Putney Bridge, across the Thames and on to Wimbledon. At East Putney, it was joined by a connection from the Clapham Junction to Barnes line. This connection still exists, albeit reduced to single line, but the occasional trains using it do not stop at what are now just Underground stations.

RIGHT: East Putney station on a card published by Hutchinson & Co. of Wimbledon and dating from 1907 or 1908. The line had now been electrified and a train bound for High Street (Kensington) is running in from the south. The L&SWR platforms can just be seen again on the left. Regular Southern Railway services on the line ceased in 1941, although it was not until 1990 that the line to Wimbledon was actually transferred to London Transport, now part of Transport for London.

No. 2002.   PUTNEY:—EAST PUTNEY STATION

The Station, Southfields, (Down Line)   Fuller's Photo Series.

LEFT: At Southfields, the station was built with just an island platform, which was generous in width and with plenty of cover. We have already noted on numerous occasions the Edwardian penchant for covering everything in advertising but that on the risers for the stairs, for the Southfields Picture Palace, probably takes the biscuit! The view is looking south and picks up a poster at the end of the platform advertising the Queens Hotel in Westcliff-on-Sea. The station was built almost beneath the crossroads where Wimbledon Park Road met Augustus Road – heading off to the left here – and Replingham Road – to the right – hence the rather restricted site, which all remains much the same today. Published in 1911, the card is part of Fuller's Photo Series.

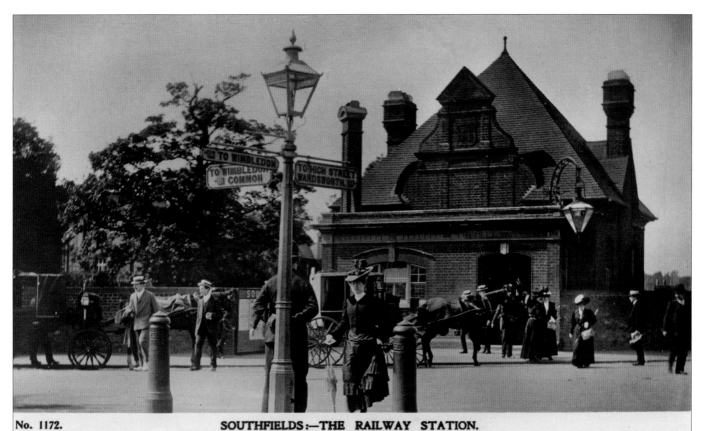

No. 1172. SOUTHFIELDS:—THE RAILWAY STATION.

ABOVE: The road level entrance to Southfields station, with every indication that a train has recently called. Opened by the L&SWR on 3rd June 1889, main line trains have not called at the station since 1941 and it is now a part of the District line; the building remains. Used in October 1907, the card was again published by Hutchinson & Co. of Wimbledon. Is that policeman actually leaning on the lamp post and note the lovely set of finger signs above his head.

BELOW: From the same year and publisher, this view is looking north at Wimbledon Park, the last station to be visited on our tour of the Underground (and our third call in Wimbledon!). Men are working on the Up line on the right, which may account for the fact that the train appears to be working wrong road – High Street is shown as the destination and the two lamps make this look like the front of the train. Again built with an island platform served from an entrance above on Arthur Road, apart from modern lighting and a lack of posters on the end wall, there is little change to the station today.

No. 1157. WIMBLEDON PARK:—RAILWAY STATION

The Edwardian and early King George V periods saw a number of large exhibitions held in London. The best known of these is perhaps the Franco-British Exhibition of 1908, in connection with which this souvenir map card of the London Electrified network was produced. The main line termini were also shown but the routes of the railways serving them were not, whilst all of the bridges over the Thames were named. Apart from that, four 'attractions' were also marked – the Tower of London, St. Paul's cathedral, Madame Tussauds and Lord's cricket ground. The card is anonymous and its origins remain unclear but it is presumed that the various Tube railways were behind its publication. It is therefore regarded as an Underground official card and has been given the reference UDG-020.

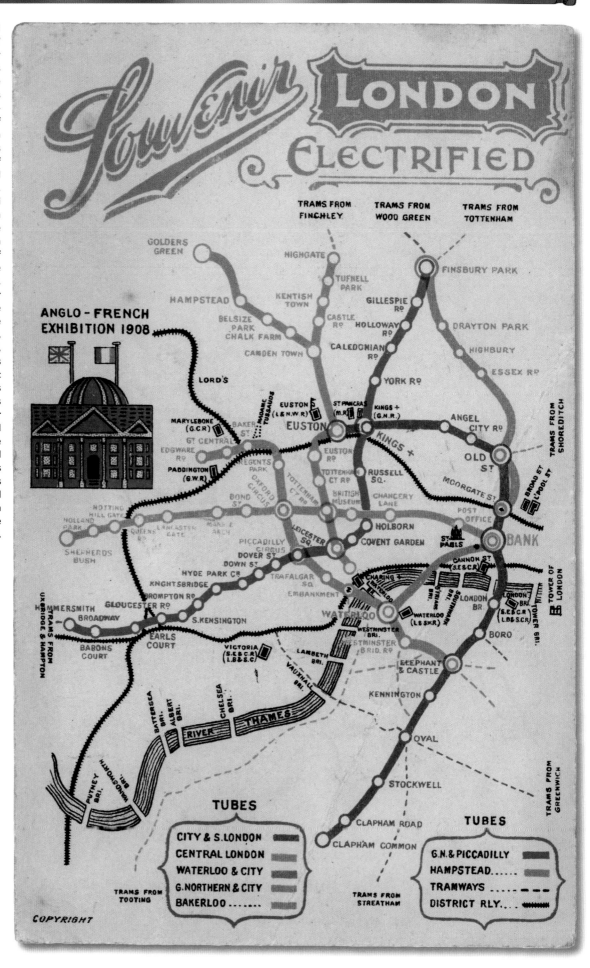

FRANCO BRITISH EXHIBITION "LONDON 1908".

15 EXHIBITIONS

ABOVE AND RIGHT: Several of the major railways had stands at the Franco-British Exhibition and produced postcards of the event. Here we see the Midland Railway stand and attendant, promoting heavily the picturesque scenery through which the line passed, particularly in the Derbyshire Peak District. The back of the card has the correspondence space printed with statistics for the company in 1907, along with a further plug for the pleasures of travel with the Midland. MR-129.

POST CARD.

THIS SPACE FOR COMMUNICATION.   ADDRESS ONLY.

MIDLAND RAILWAY, the Best Route for Comfortable Travel and Picturesque Scenery.

Photochrom Co., Ltd., London and Detroit, U.S.A. Printed in England.

Midland Railway Statistics, 1907.

Total Revenue - - - £13,061,598
Lines owned (Miles) - - - 1,688
Lines partly owned (Miles) - - 660
Carriage Stock - - - 5,457
Wagon Stock - - - 117,833
Stations - - - 603
Total Number of Employees - 75,004

Passengers travelling for pleasure or on business in Great Britain or to and from the Continent are respectfully informed that the Midland Railway Company's express trains and connections serve most of the places of industrial and tourist interest in Great Britian and North of Ireland, and comfortable and expeditious travel is ensured by this route. Beautiful scenery. The best restaurant service.

POST CARD

L. & N. W. RLY.

Journey Times—

(FOR ADDRESS ONLY.)

2d. per set of six different cards. Over 8½ millions sold.

EUSTON AND   Hrs. Mins.
ABERDEEN - - in 11 15
BARROW-IN-FURNESS ,, 6 7
BELFAST - - ,, 11 55
BIRKENHEAD - ,, 4 15
BIRMINGHAM - ,, 2 0
BLACKBURN - ,, 4 39
BLACKPOOL - ,, 5 31
BOLTON - - ,, 4 6
CHESTER - ,, 3 36
COVENTRY - ,, 1 43
DUBLIN - - ,, 9 0
EDINBURGH - ,, 8 0
GLASGOW - ,, 8 0
INVERNESS - ,, 13 30
LIVERPOOL - ,, 3 35
MANCHESTER - ,, 3 30
NORTHAMPTON - ,, 1 30
OBAN - - ,, 12 55
ROCHDALE - ,, 4 25
SHREWSBURY - ,, 3 12
WARRINGTON - ,, 3 34
WOLVERHAMPTON - ,, 2 28

BREAKFAST, LUNCHEON, DINING & SLEEPING CARS. Best Permanent Way in the World.

L & N.W. & CALEDONIAN RAILWAYS' EXHIBIT FRANCO-BRITISH EXHIBITION. 1908.

ABOVE AND RIGHT: The London & North Western and Caledonian railways jointly promoted the West Coast route, the L&NWR producing this card illustrating the joint stand. Note the postcards on the table in the near corner. To the right can be seen the Lancashire & Yorkshire Railway stand but it seems that this company did not have any cards specially produced for the exhibition. LNW-759.

The Great Northern Railway displayed locomotives old and new at the Imperial International Exhibition held at the White City in 1909. Partly in view on the left is Ivatt 'Atlantic' No. 1442, which had been built the previous year and representative of what were the top express engines on the GNR before the introduction of the Gresley 'Pacifics'. On the right is Stirling 'Single' No. 1, built at Doncaster in 1870 and an example of what had been the GNR's top link express motive power until the arrival of the 'Atlantics'. So successful were the 'Single' 4-2-2s that batches of them in various forms were constructed up until 1895 but they were then quickly superseded by the 'Atlantic' 4-4-2s, with withdrawals having commenced by the turn of the century. No. 1 had been taken out of service the year before the exhibition but had been earmarked for preservation. It was restored to working order for a time in 1938 and today may be seen as a static exhibit at the National Railway Museum in York. After Grouping, the 'Atlantic' became L&NER No. 1442 in 1924 and then No. 2872 in early 1946 but was withdrawn a year later, just prior to Nationalisation of the railways. The track formed part of the exhibit, with boards in front of the 'bowler' indicating that the permanent way beneath No. 1 was the standard for that laid in 1870, whilst that beneath No. 1442 represented the way track was now laid in 1909. The GNR did not issue a postcard of the event but E. Pouteau published this view which also just shows a corner of the L&NWR stand on the left.

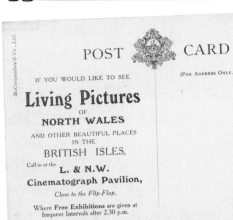

LEFT AND BELOW: The Imperial International Exhibition presented another chance for the L&NWR and CR to get together and promote the West Coast Route. Again it was the former who produced a postcard of the stand, the back including a note of the 'Living Pictures' to be seen at the 'L.& N.W. Cinematograph Pavilion, *Close to the Flip-Flap*'. In the stamp space is the usual advertisement, 2d. per set of six different cards, with over 9 million sold, which gives a good clue as to why so many of the L&NWR cards are easily found today. LNW-760

RIGHT AND ABOVE: One of the smaller railways to stand at the Imperial International Exhibition in 1909 was the Furness Railway, who made great use of the Lake District scenery in their publicity. This is one of a couple of postcards for this exhibition produced for the company by Raphael Tuck, the timescale for which, from photographing the completed stand to having the cards available, must have been quite short. The reverse of the card, above, is identical to that of the 1910 card below. FR-154.

LEFT: In 1910, the Japan-British Exhibition was held at White City, where the Furness Railway also had a stand, with three different cards of it being produced for them by Tucks. Here we can see the Furness were drawing attention to the Barrow-in-Furness area with a map indicating sites available for business purposes. As might be expected, however, the major part of the display concentrated on the attractions of the Lake District – 'The English Lake Land'; the Swiss Lakes were popular with Continental travellers at this time and this was the Furness promoting similar scenic attractions much closer to home. Surprisingly there was apparently nothing from the L&NWR for this show in the way of a postcard. FR-157.

POST CARD

M Corquodale & Co., Limited.

The "Rocket" Engine.

This celebrated engine was built in 1829 and was the most successful locomotive competing in the famous "Rainhill" trial in October of that year. The total weight of engine and tender was 7.45 tons. The model shown on the L. & N. W. Stand in the Machinery Hall at the White City is an exact copy, shown standing on the original permanent way (fish bellied type) fixed across the diagonal of square pieces of stone by means of cast iron chairs.

(FOR ADDRESS ONLY.)

Buy the
L. & N. W. Series
of Pictorial
Postcards.
2d. per set of six
different cards.
Over 10 millions
sold.

Travel to SCOTLAND by the
West Coast Royal Mail Route.

Over the Border in under 6 hours
from Euston Station.

LEFT AND BELOW: On 22nd June 1911, George V was crowned King so of course there was an exhibition as part of the celebrations. Once again the L&NWR had a stand, although again there is no known card showing this. They did, however, produce another postcard showing one of their latest express engines alongside a model of *Rocket*, which was on display on their stand and no doubt this card was available for sale there too. Note that the total number of L&NWR cards sold is now shown as 10 million. The express engine is No. 2155, a 4-4-0 of the 'George V' Class, named *W.C. Brocklehurst*. New in November 1910, No. 2155 lasted until December 1936, when it was withdrawn as LM&SR No. 5326. The engines are seen posed at Crewe Works and on the reverse of the card, produced as were most of the company's cards by McCorquodale & Co. Ltd, carried a small advert for the joint L&NWR/CR West Coast Royal Mail Route. LNW-761.

THE "ROCKET"
BUILT 1829
AND ONE OF THE
L.&N.W. SUPERHEATED LOCOMOTIVES
BUILT 1911.

THIS MODEL
OF THE "ROCKET"
IS EXHIBITED
ON THE L.&N.W STAND
AT THE
CORONATION EXHIBITION

RIGHT: The final exhibition to be visited took place in 1914, when the Anglo-American Exposition was staged at Shepherds Bush. For this event the Great Eastern Railway produced a couple of cards, printer unknown, depicting part of their display. This rather austere card shows a reproduction of part of The Strangers' Hall in Norwich, the other being a mock up of a section of the interior of one of their Channel steamers. These cards were presumably available to visitors to the stand and some examples were also printed for correspondence use by the Superintendent of the Line, although the reverse of this one is blank apart from the normal 'Post Card' title and stamp square. GE-335.

ANGLO-AMERICAN
EXPOSITION,
SHEPHERDS BUSH,
LONDON, 1914.

The
Great Eastern Railway
Company's Exhibit
in the Transport Section.
Reproduction of an
East Anglian Ancient
Building
(The Strangers' Hall,
Norwich, 14th Century).

To finish this section, we return to Earl's Court for this circa 1904 view of the Great Wheel that was erected for the Empire of India Exhibition in July 1895. Construction of the wheel, which was modelled on the original Ferris wheel built for the 1893 World's Columbian Exposition in Chicago, USA, began in March 1894. It was built by Maudslay, Sons & Field of Greenwich and was 308 feet in height with a diameter of 270 feet. It is perhaps best compared with the 'Eye' wheels that have proliferated around the world in the last couple of decades, having forty 'cars' each with a capacity for forty persons. It was taken out of use after the Imperial Austrian Exhibition of 1906 and demolished the following year, by which time it was estimated to have been ridden by $2^1/_2$ million passengers. Strictly, it had no railway connection and none of the exhibitions at which it was used are known to have produced any railway related postcards, so its appearance within these pages is tenuous. However, its inclusion is perhaps justified by the L&SWR tank engine standing on the District Railway's double track spur connecting Earl's Court and West Brompton stations, and by the hugely interesting and historic nature of the view. Note the railwaymen's allotments in the foreground. The line is still in use today but this section was hidden when the Earl's Court Exhibition Centre, opened in 1937, was partly built over the top of it. This was somewhat controversially demolished in 2015 and the site is now earmarked for a major residential and retail development.

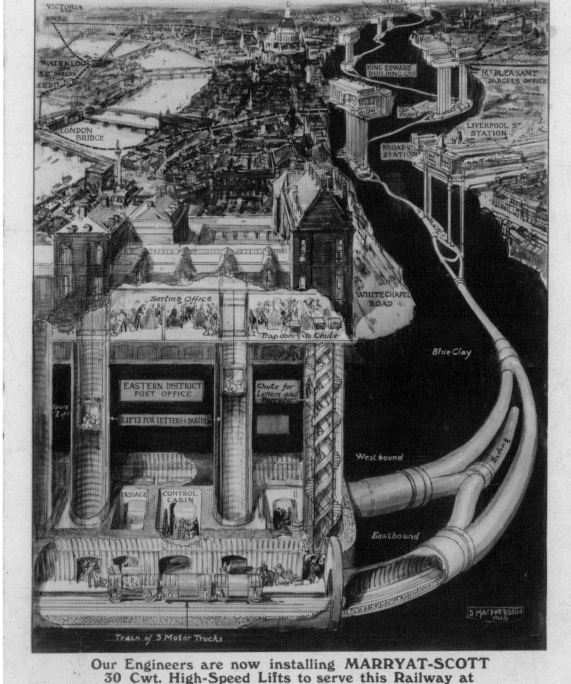

To complete the tour of London's railways we move away from the main passenger lines and start here with a look at the Post Office Railway. This opened in 1927, so it is really just outside the pre-Grouping period of the main lines covered but its inclusion is justified by the fact that planning for the railway actually began in 1911, with construction commencing in February 1915. However, the privations of the First World War brought this to a halt in 1917 and it was not until 1924 that work was sufficiently far advanced for track laying to commence. This view, on an advertising card for Marryat-Scott Ltd's high-speed lifts, gives an interesting cross-section. It is an oversize card (115 by 165 mm), and is a photograph of a sectional drawing by D. MacPherson, which is dated 1916 below the signature. The postcard was printed by Lilywhite and has been seen used by the lift company in 1927 and 1929. To get round postal regulations, the card was headed 'PRINTED MATTER' on the reverse rather than 'POST CARD', thus saving a halfpenny on postage. The picture was originally published, date unknown, in *The Graphic*, a weekly paper that ceased publication in 1932. Marryat-Scott Ltd were formed in 1919, with the business being taken over by Kone in 1979.

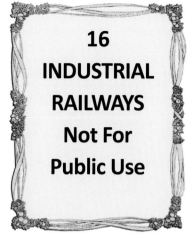

16
INDUSTRIAL
RAILWAYS
Not For
Public Use

ABOVE LEFT: Prior to the opening of the Post Office Railway, mail for the major central London sorting centre here at Mount Pleasant had to be carried to and from the various termini by road. This circa 1906 card shows the arrival of parcel mail, delivered in early motor vans. The rather stiff poses come from the lengthy exposure required with the cumbersome, tripod-mounted plate glass negative cameras of the period. Much of this traffic ceased with the opening of the underground mail railway.

LEFT: The original rolling stock provided for the railway in 1927 proved prone to derailments and was replaced with new units in 1930, of which No. 760 seen here was part of the first batch built. They utilised the electrical equipment from the 1927 stock and some lasted until the line closed in 2003. No. 760 became No. 37 when new stock was introduced in 1984 and is today preserved at the private Beeches Light Railway in Buckinghamshire. The Post Office Railway re-opened as a tourist line in September 2017.

RIGHT: Again stretching things a little, this view is really just outside the area being explored but is an unusual one, showing LCC No. 1. at the London County Council's Charlton Repair Depot, which was situated alongside the SE&CR's Angerstein Wharf Branch. The picture was taken on 28th March 1931 but the engine had been here since the depot opened in March 1909. Built by Andrew Barclay in 1904 at their Caledonia Works in Kilmarnock, Works No. 991, it was originally delivered to the LCC Works Department at Abbey Wood and named *Plumstead*. The engine was modified to allow it to shunt the trams that were serviced here – note the lack of normal buffers – and was scrapped a couple of years after being photographed, following takeover of the depot by the London Paasssnger Transport Board. This is another LPC card.

RIGHT: Just to the north of Angerstein Wharf, alongside the River Thames and now back within the our area of study, was the vast East Greenwich gas works of the South Metropolitan Gas Company. As the only significant rail-served industrial site within the central London area for which cards have been found, we will finish our tour with a selection of views covering it in detail. The site chosen for the works was Greenwich Marsh, where the bulk of construction was carried out between 1883 and 1886. This circa 1908 view shows a part of the huge block of Retort Houses, each gravity fed by a high level line bringing laden side-tipping coal wagons in, which were then run back out at ground level after being emptied. In the foreground is the engine shed and workshops, with the two enormous gas holders on Tunnel Road in the background.

LEFT: The volumes of coal and coke to be shifted required an extensive internal railway system, with a fleet of tank locomotives to do the work. The engines were all small saddle tanks to cope with the sharp curves. A group of workmen pose in front of No. 6, built by Hawthorn, Leslie in 1895, Works No. 2335, which spent its entire career here, being sold for scrap in 1955. Behind is again part of the Retort Houses building. The card was an unusual production by the large and well known national publishers Valentine & Co. Ltd in 1907 or 1908.

RIGHT: Another of the Hawthorn, Leslie tanks is dwarfed beside the coke sales hoppers. The coke would have come by rail from the Retort Houses in tipper wagons and was stored for sale to local merchants. Several drays are in evidence ready to pick up a load. The locomotives did not have bunkers, with a small amount of coal able to be stored on the footplate, so they were coaled regularly from the piles seen here on the ground. Probably dating from a similar period to the previous two cards, it was published anonymously. When first established, the railway system here was completely autonomous but some time prior to the First World War it was connected to the Angerstein Wharf Branch by a mile long line.

THE JETTY. S.M. GASWORKS EAST GREENWICH.

A south-easterly view of the substantial river jetty by which shipborne coal from the Northumberland coalfield was delivered for the gas works, with a train of tipper wagons just visible on the left being loaded. In the right foreground is the works clock tower and offices. The jetty survived the closure of the works for many years, even after the site had been cleared and used for the construction of the Millenium Dome, now the O2 Arena, but it has now been largely removed, although two small sections of it were retained, one of which now holds the Anthony Gormley artwork *Quantum Cloud*. A new lower jetty was built alongside these remains, which forms the North Greenwich Pier for Transport for London's River Bus service. The rest of the gas works site has been redeveloped for housing and retail, and is served by a new underground station on the Jubilee Line, named North Greenwich and not to be confused with the first North Greenwich station, on the opposite bank of the river (see page 76).

Peckett 0-4-0ST No. 17 stands at the head of a train of tipper wagons. The oversize buffers on the engine were to prevent locking on the sharp curves with the much smaller wagons. As well as the cast numberplate on the cab side, note the plate with painted number affixed to the chimney. The date of this and the following two East Greenwich views, published by the Locomotive Publishing Co., is not known but the cards are from the early 1930s and the views are probably contemporary. Although they are thus outside the period we are looking at, much of the scene here had changed little over the preceding twenty years and the views largely tie in with a 1916 OS map. The wagons had changed, however, the metal-bodied tipping hoppers we see here having replaced the wooden-bodied wagons used previously, one of which can be seen in the foreground of the first picture, top left. Loaded with coal, they would be propelled up to the high level and then run down by gravity into the retort house and tipped by hand into the retort coal store. Each store could hold 6,600 tons of coal. No. 17 was new from Peckett's in 1912 (Works No. 1286) and spent its enture career here at Greenwich, being scrapped in July 1959.

ABOVE: A general view of the works, again probably in the early 1930s, looking south. A train of tipper wagons stands by the signal box partly obscuring it with steam. The large retort building is on the right, beyond the ramp which led to the high level tracks and to the coal jetty. The new looking building in the centre was a recent provision for servicing and housing the locomotives, replacing the sheds seen previously.

BELOW: Much of the works railway at East Greenwich was raised above ground and this view is looking in the opposite direction, up the ramp. The raised lines were another reason for small engines, weight being a factor. There is a saddle tank either side of the signal box, and behind the centre signal the South Met's clock tower can just be seen. The signalling was the other major change from the earlier pictures, this being a recent addition to the system at the date of these views. Note also the different design of side tipping wagons on show here, similar to the wooden sided wagons but with metal bodies. The River Thames is just to the right and the high level line can be seen heading over the water to the jetty. The change to natural gas saw the cessation of gas production here in 1968, with complete closure of the works occurring in 1976 when the by-products plant was also shut down.

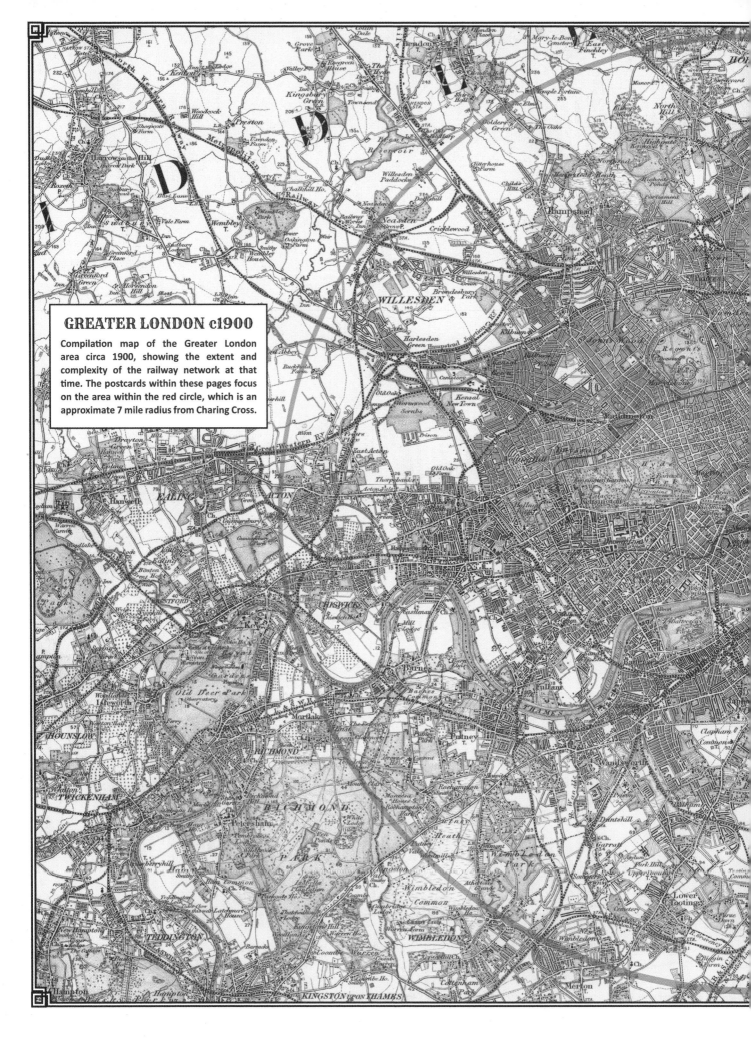

GREATER LONDON c1900

Compilation map of the Greater London area circa 1900, showing the extent and complexity of the railway network at that time. The postcards within these pages focus on the area within the red circle, which is an approximate 7 mile radius from Charing Cross.